THE CUSTOMER-BASE AUDIT

The First Step on the Journey to

CUSTOMER CENTRICITY

THE CUSTOMER-BASE AUDIT

PETER FADER BRUCE HARDIE MICHAEL ROSS

WHARTON SCHOOL PRESS
Philadelphia

Published by Wharton School Press
The Wharton School
University of Pennsylvania
3620 Locust Walk
300 Steinberg Hall-Dietrich Hall
Philadelphia, PA 19104
Email: whartonschoolpress@wharton.upenn.edu
Website: wsp.wharton.upenn.edu/

Ebook ISBN: 978-1-61363-159-1
Paperback ISBN: 978-1-61363-160-7
Hardcover ISBN: 978-1-61363-161-4

Contents

Acknowledgments

The authors would like to thank Matt Burgess and Jennifer Day for creating a clean dataset on which they could perform all the analyses presented in this book, Eva Ascarza for her incredibly detailed and thoughtful feedback on an early draft, and Whitney Braunstein and Michael Braun for introducing Michael to Bruce and Pete.

Introduction
Why a Customer-Base Audit?

In the course of the American Airlines Group Q3 2015 results earnings call, Scott Kirby, then the president of American Airlines, made the following comment:

> A statistic that when I told people they find somewhat amazing is that 87% of the people that have flown American Airlines in the last year flew us only one time. So 87% of our unique customers fly us one time for a year or less, and they represent over 50% of our revenue.

We were surprised to read this. The numbers themselves were not surprising; any serious student of customer buying behavior would expect such a pattern. What surprised us was the fact that such a senior executive knew them in the first place.

As a senior executive, you will be very familiar with your organization's key financial statements and monthly management reports. You have spent countless hours discussing budgets and expenditures. Focusing on the top line of the income statement, you will probably have looked at sales by product line and geography. You quite possibly have looked at product profitability as part of a product line rationalization exercise.

But how much time have you spent reflecting on the fact that these revenues are generated by customers pulling out their wallets and paying for your products and services? What do you really know about this primary source of your organization's (inward) operating cash flow?[1]

Consider the following questions:

- How many customers does your firm have? How many customers do you *really* have?
- How do these customers differ in terms of their value to the firm? For example, how many one-time buyers did you have last year? How many customers accounted for half of your revenue last year?
- How many customers who bought your products last year can be expected to buy from you this year?
- What proportion of your sales this past year came from new versus existing customers?
- On average, what proportion of your new customers have made a second purchase within three months of their first-ever purchase? Within six months? A year?
- Which of your products are most appealing to your most valuable customers?

If you are struggling to answer these questions, you are in good company. In our experience, most senior executives are unable to do so, regardless of whether their organization is primarily B2B or B2C, sells products or services, or is a for-profit or nonprofit.

Why is this the case? It reflects a fundamental failing in the reporting systems and structures of most organizations. It reflects a failure to have a true customer-centric mindset, even by many firms that claim to be customer centric.

We expect that some people, lurking in various parts of your organization, are conducting the analyses that can provide the answers to some of these questions. But it is rare to find them being pulled together in one place, let alone making their way to senior management. Yet without such a basic understanding of the foundations of the behavior of the firm's primary source of (inward) operating cash flow, how can you be expected to ask the right questions and make informed decisions?

Enter the Customer-Base Audit

We believe that there is a set of fundamental analyses that are foundational for any executive wanting to gain an understanding of the health of their organization's revenue and profit streams and the feasibility of their growth plans.

We call this the customer-base audit.

A customer-base audit is a systematic review of the buying behavior of a firm's customers using data captured by its transaction systems. The objective is to provide an understanding of how customers differ in their buying behavior and how their buying behavior evolves over time.

It is important to note that we are not talking about "knowing the customer" through the lens of traditional market research. We are not interested in the demographic profile of our customers. We are not interested in their attitudes. We are interested in understanding their actual buying behavior.

Who would want to look at the results of such an audit?

- Senior management teams and boards that recognize that to really understand the top line, they need to examine it through the lens of the customer.
- A CEO who wishes to embark on a journey of making the firm truly customer centric.
- Groups undertaking a due-diligence exercise as part of an M&A or investment decision that recognize the importance of understanding the health of the firm's customer base.
- A CMO wanting to get their team to start taking a more data-based approach to their planning and decision making.

A nonprofit supported by charitable donations may want to perform the associated analyses for both its financial supporters and the people it serves through its charitable activities. The same applies to two-sided markets such as Airbnb that often view both their constituencies (hosts and guests) as different kinds of customers.

We agree with the definition of analytics as "the discipline that applies logic and mathematics to data to provide insights for making better decisions."[2] It is common to talk of four types of analytics capabilities: descriptive ("what is currently happening or has happened?"), diagnostic ("why did it happen?"), predictive ("what will happen?"), and prescriptive ("what should we do?").

The general view among business leaders is that firms progress from simple (descriptive) to sophisticated (prescriptive) analytics engagement, with the derived value increasing as the firm adopts more sophisticated tools. We disagree with this view. At a time when everyone is caught up in the hype surrounding machine learning and artificial intelligence and believing that "sophisticated equals better," the customer-base audit is unashamedly descriptive (and, to a much lesser extent, diagnostic) in its approach. Time and again, we have seen how the insights derived from these descriptive analyses can have a profound impact on a firm's operations.

It is important to note that we are not repackaging the idea of a marketing dashboard. To start, most marketing dashboards do not have the customer as the central unit of analysis, which is rather ironic. Moreover, the customer-base audit is not a "marketing" endeavor. While it will surely be of interest to people working in roles associated with the marketing function, our primary audience is senior management (think CEO and CFO, not only the CMO).

More fundamentally, the dashboard metaphor implies constant feedback and immediate action. A customer-base audit is all about gaining a fundamental understanding of the behavior of the firm's customers. It involves a serious engagement with the fact that revenue is generated by customers pulling out their wallets and paying for a firm's products and services, and that any attempt to think about a firm's revenue streams must start with a good understanding of how customers differ and how their behavior evolves over time.

Why are firms not undertaking the types of analyses that would answer these questions on a more systematic basis? There are several reasons. First, most managers have not been exposed to such analyses. If you have never been exposed to the idea of thinking about the customer as the unit of analysis when analyzing your firm's revenues and profits, how can you be expected to ask such questions in the first place?

Another reason for failing to undertake these types of analyses is technological barriers, be they real or imagined: "We don't have the data," or "It's too difficult to get the data." That may have been true 20 years ago, but now it is a rather hollow excuse. (If you are working in a digitally native company, you have no excuse!)

If you are over a certain age, you grew up in a world where, even if the data were accessible, such analysis was expensive. You probably had to hire consultants to do it. It is much easier these days. Analyses we undertook 20 years ago, which required days or weeks of expert analyst time using complex software with expensive licenses, can now be done by someone with minimal training on easy-to-use software, much of which is open-source. If you have a small transaction database (fewer than one million transaction records), you can even do the analyses using spreadsheet software (such as Microsoft Excel), an exercise we do with our MBA students.

About This Book

This is not your typical business book. We are going to take a deep dive into detailed customer data. We are going to explore a set of fundamental analyses that we hope will change the perspective from which you think about what underpins the performance of your firm.

If you have read either of Pete's two prior books, *Customer Centricity* and *The Customer Centricity Playbook*, you might be wondering how this book is different. In many ways, this book can be viewed as a prequel to those books. Similar to those books, we define a customer-centric firm as one that:

- views the customer as the fundamental unit of analysis;
- has (customer) acquisition, retention, and development at the core of its (organic) growth accounting framework;
- makes decisions through the lens of (long-term) customer profitability; and
- recognizes—and acts on—the fact that not all customers are equal.

But Pete's two books focus a great deal on the *future*. He emphasizes the use of predictive models and forward-looking concepts such as *customer lifetime value* (CLV). However, before we look to the future and start running such models, there is plenty we can learn from the *present*—and the trajectory from the recent past—to guide our decision making and to prioritize our analytical endeavors.

Exploring the results (and implications) of a customer-base audit is a natural and valuable starting point for many management teams on their journey to be customer centric, as they move from mere talk to grappling with what it means for how they think about their business.

Regardless of the size and sophistication of your team of analysts—one or two people with standard Excel and database querying skills or a large group with PhDs in statistics and computer science—you can undertake a customer-base audit. In our experience, serious engagement with the issues raised via the audit has played an important role in getting skeptics on board with the idea of being more analytics- and data-driven.

If you have looked ahead in the book, you will have seen that there are lots of figures and tables. And that may be a bit scary. But have no fear: First, we will make everything clear and practical, even as we get deeper into the data. Second, that bit of discomfort is a good wake-up call. No senior executive can be financially illiterate. Anyone without the background will acquire basic accounting and finance literacy as they rise through the ranks of an organization.

Likewise, we are now operating in an environment where you cannot afford to be data illiterate; you cannot be scared off by such analyses. It is important that engaging with these types of analyses becomes second nature. Our goal is to provide a gentle introduction to a set of analyses that you can then have an analyst in your organization produce for you and your firm.

Why We Wrote This Book

Pete and Bruce started working together in the fall of 1989, when Pete was an assistant professor of marketing at the Wharton School and Bruce had just started the PhD program there. During their first decade of working together, they spent a lot of time using consumer panel data (as collected by market research firms such as IRI, Kantar, and Nielsen) to develop data-based brand choice models and new product sales forecasting models. As e-commerce took off in the late 1990s, they turned their attention to the development of predictive models of customer buying behavior that made use of the data in a firm's customer transaction databases. Over the years, they have developed a number of key customer analytics tools for computing customer lifetime value (CLV) that have been used by thousands of data scientists and researchers around the world.

Around the time Bruce and Pete were starting to work with customer transaction data, Michael left McKinsey & Company and cofounded figleaves.com, a UK-based online lingerie retailer. Having studied mathematics at Cambridge, he was comfortable with data but had no immediate sense of what types of analyses he should undertake to gain actionable insights into the behavior of his firm's customers. Working from first principles, he identified some basic analyses of the type presented in this book and has refined them in his subsequent start-up and consulting activities. Bruce and Michael now co-teach a course at the London Business School that covers many of these concepts and methods.

The types of analyses presented in this book have become second nature to us. And we know from working with firms that the analyses we group together under the heading of the customer-base audit can have a profound impact on an organization. However, whenever we have been asked for further readings on the topic, we have not been able to come up with a simple reading list. Some of the ideas are contained in obscure academic articles that are not easy to read. Some practitioner-oriented books touch on these topics, but do not pursue them with the full depth and rigor that they merit.

The absence of any single comprehensive book or other resource that lays out all of this content was a critical "missing link" in the journey toward customer centricity. We decided to address this important issue, and you now have the results of our efforts in your hands.

Chapter 1

Setting the Scene

Let us revisit the first question we posed in the introduction: How many customers do you have?

If you are having trouble providing an answer, you are far from alone. We have long stopped being surprised by the inability of most CEOs, let alone CMOs, to do so.

If you can answer that question, let us ask you some more:

- How confident are you in the number? Would an external auditor come up with the same answer?
- Would your colleagues in other functional areas give the same number?

Unless you are working for an insurance company, a telecommunications firm, or some other company where subscriptions lie at the heart of the revenue model, it is most likely that you are not very confident in your answer to the "How many customers?" question. And you probably have doubts that there would be strong agreement across functional areas. How can this be?

The primary reason for the inability to answer the first question is that many firms simply do not prioritize this number, in spite of any claims about being "customer centric." Difficulty with the other questions arises from the problematic nature of the term "customer" and the failure of most firms to come to grips with it. As we shall see, even the dictionary definition of "customer" can be problematic.

What and Who Is a Customer?

Consider the following vignette. Try to answer the question "For which of these organizations is Sarah a customer?"

> With an hour to spare before she boards a United Airlines flight to London, Sarah is sitting in one of the Starbucks outlets at O'Hare International Airport in Chicago with a grande latte in her hand. In front of her is her Lenovo ThinkPad, which she purchased two years ago. (This notebook PC runs Windows.) She is checking her Gmail account, having just paid for an hour's Wi-Fi access via a Boingo hot spot using her Visa card.
>
> At the same time, she is checking voice mail on her work phone (an iPhone purchased six months ago). Back in the UK, this is on the Vodafone network; it is currently connected to T-Mobile. Under the table is a battered Tumi roll-aboard, which she bought 11 years ago.

Now get a colleague to go through the same exercise. Do you get the same answers? Probably not. Whenever we do this exercise with our MBA students, we get a wide range of answers. Hard-core finance types tend to have a short list, while hard-core marketing types tend to come up with a longer one. So let us consider the areas of consensus: Everyone agrees that Sarah is a customer of Starbucks and Boingo.

The first disagreement typically emerges when we ask whether Sarah is a customer of Google. There is no doubt that she is a *user* of Google's services, but does that make her a customer? Many will contend she is not because she is not paying anything. The second disagreement emerges when we ask whether Sarah is a customer of Lenovo. Let us suppose she purchased the computer directly from Lenovo's online store. She made the purchase two years ago and was therefore a customer at the time. Should we still call her a customer two years later? What if the item is still under warranty? Is she still a customer?

Here are some questions to ask when coming up with a working definition of a customer for your organization. There are no absolute right or wrong answers. However, you should answer those that are relevant to your organization and its business model.

1. Is payment required for someone to be considered a customer?

This lies at the heart of any disagreement as to whether Sarah is a customer of Google. Some people will follow a dictionary definition of "customer," such as that given by Oxford Dictionaries: "a person or organization that buys goods or services from a store or business."[3] Others will want to take a broader view. This definitional issue is not just a problem faced by commercial firms that focus on revenue as a primary metric. Consider a food bank that provides food parcels to individuals and families in crisis. Are the recipients of the food parcels "customers" whose usage of the charity's services it would like to understand? While the charity may not want to use the term "customer" to describe the users of its service, it should be interested in tracking and understanding users' behavior through the types of analyses we will present in this book.

2. Does it matter who pays versus who uses? Does it matter who made the decision?

No one disagrees that Sarah is a passenger of United. But is she a customer? If told that this is a flight Sarah chose and purchased using her own money, everyone agrees that she is a customer. But what if she is being reimbursed by her employer? What if Sarah chose the flight but it was booked (and paid for) by her employer? What if she was simply given the ticket by her employer, having no choice regarding airline or schedule? Where do we draw the line between Sarah being a customer and not being a customer?

These same questions are relevant when we ask whether Sarah is a customer of Apple and Vodafone. Was her phone issued to her by her employer, or does her firm have a BYOD (bring your own device) policy? How does that affect our characterization of Sarah as a customer?

3. How long after the purchase does a customer cease to be a customer (even if they are still an owner and user)?

Had Sarah just purchased her Tumi roll-aboard, there would be agreement that she is a customer. Yet she purchased it 11 years ago, which makes many uncomfortable using the label "customer" to describe Sarah, preferring to think about purchasing in the past 12 months or the current financial year as being a requirement for that label.

4. Do we factor in any legal obligations?

Sarah purchased her computer two years ago. If you apply the term "customer" only to those individuals or organizations that have been a source of revenue in the past year, Sarah is not a customer. However, her computer came with a three-year warranty, so Lenovo does have some contractual obligation to her. Do we still want to use the word "customer" to describe such individuals or organizations?

5. Does the presence of a channel intermediary in the purchasing process stop someone from being considered a customer?

Suppose Sarah purchased her Tumi roll-aboard from a retailer. It is tempting to view the retailer as the customer, as Sarah is not immediately visible to Tumi. But perhaps such measurement challenges should not get in the way of defining what and who is a customer.

There may be additional questions you need to ask when coming up with a working definition of a customer for your organization. The key takeaway is that defining a "customer" is not as obvious as it may first seem.

Different Definitions for Different Purposes

Can you come up with a clear, single definition for your firm? Maybe not. And maybe, after thinking through all of these challenging questions, it is too much to expect every firm to be able to do so.

Should Sarah be considered a customer of United if the ticket was given to her by her employer? If you work in customer service, you may want to say yes. If you are a key account manager, you would probably say her employer is the customer.

Consider those attending executive education courses at institutions such as the Wharton School and London Business School. Are the participants the customers, or are their employers the customers? The answer is probably both. What constitutes an appropriate definition of "customer" will depend on the questions being asked.

If you are FedEx, some people in the organization (such as customer service) will care about the end recipient to whom the package is being shipped. Do we want to think of both the sender and the recipient of a package as customers, albeit different "types" of customers? Similarly, if you are a hotel, you might be interested in the behavior of both the "booker" and the "stayer," which in many settings will be different individuals.

Firms faced with such a hierarchy of possible customer definitions or different "types" of customers may find it interesting to conduct many of the analyses that we will be exploring at all levels and for all customer types. Companies that understand this will be very careful in their use of the term "customer." In fact, they may avoid using the term altogether. Let us go back to Sarah's use of her Visa card. Is she a customer of Visa? The card she used is not issued by Visa but by a bank. She has a relationship with the issuing bank, but no direct relationship with Visa. She is what Visa calls an account holder. Visa has two distinct groups of "customers": the financial institutions that issue the cards and the merchants that accept the cards, with whom it has a direct relationship.

The bottom line is that for many firms there is no clean and simple definition of what constitutes a customer. The important thing is to be clear about your terms and consistent in your usage of the terms.

How Many Customers Do You Have?

It is not uncommon for organizations to publish details about the number of customers they have. But these numbers should be treated with care. Let us consider two examples.

- Transport for London states that the London Underground (better known as the Tube) has 1.35 billion passengers per annum. Does this mean that about 17% of the world's population travels on the Tube in a year? Of course not. Transport for London is reporting the number of trips made; it is not reporting the number of *unique* individuals that traveled on the Tube. An office worker taking the Tube to and from work, five days a week, for 46 weeks of the year, would be counted as 460 passengers.
- Sadler's Wells Theatre, a major London performing arts venue dedicated to dance, noted in its 2017–18 Annual Review that "we presented 649 performances to over 529,700 people across our three London auditoria." That represents the total number of seats occupied across the financial year but is not the number of *unique* individuals who attended a performance in that time period.

If you are going to talk about the number of customers you have, it should be the number of unique customers. Your ability to do so will depend on the measurement systems you have in place, your definition of a customer, and your channel structures.

Let us think about those individuals using the Tube. Some will be using a season ticket or registered Oyster card. Transport for London knows the identity of such passengers and can track their behavior. Other passengers will use an unregistered Oyster card or their contactless debit or credit card to pay for their trip. While

Transport for London can track the behavior of such passengers, it does not know their identity. And then there will be some passengers using paper tickets whose identity and behavior over time cannot be tracked. Most retailers face a similar mix of known; known but anonymous (e.g., "tokenized" credit card data); and truly anonymous customers (e.g., those who always pay with cash).

The ability to track customer behavior can also depend on the definition of "customer." Consider a dance enthusiast who purchases a total of 19 tickets across seven performances at Sadler's Wells. They take a total of eight different friends to these various performances. How many customers are represented here? Definitely not 19. But do we have one (the ticket buyer) or nine customers (the ticket buyer and their friends)? The answer will depend on how we define "customer." The finance director will probably be happy to say one, which implies the definition of "customer" includes some notion of payment. But anyone reporting to arts-funding authorities will want to say nine, which implies the definition of "customer" includes the idea of attendance but not necessarily payment. The challenge is how to uniquely identify those individuals.

So, even if you can agree on what and who is a customer, measuring how many customers you have can be a challenge. Is the customer, as defined, visible in your systems? Can each transaction be tied to a specific customer? For many firms, the answer to these two questions is yes, which makes it very easy to determine the number of customers it has. However, as illustrated above, it is more problematic for other organizations. In recognizing the value of data on customer-level buying behavior, many firms are making major investments in systems so as to make the customer explicitly visible in their reporting.

A supermarket's point-of-sale system gives it great information on what is in each shopping basket, but no sense of how different shopping baskets are related to each other over time. Why do supermarkets invest in the development of loyalty programs? So that they can identify the customer associated with each shopping basket and act on the insights gained from analyzing customer behavior.

Firms with no direct connection to their ultimate customer can face issues of customer visibility. Going back to Sarah, how can she be made visible to Tumi? Historically, warranty registration has been one mechanism for identifying the final customer when (durable) products are sold via intermediaries.

Consumer packaged goods (CPG) companies have always had this problem. However, since the 1940s, syndicated market research firms have offered consumer panel services that track the buying behavior of a sample of households. While only a very small fraction of the firm's customers are represented in a panel, their behavior can still be analyzed to gain very useful insights. (In fact, some of the analyses we explore in this book will be familiar to those readers who have used consumer panel data reports in their work.)

The past decade has seen the emergence of data providers that process anonymized credit card purchasing data, thereby giving companies "known but anonymous" customer data for a portion of their customer base. Once again, though this is not the same as having your own data on customer buying behavior, you can gain a number of useful insights using such data sources.

Conclusion

Regardless of how a firm defines the customer, it should desire and prioritize the need to understand customers' behavior at a granular level. That is the overarching motivation for this book. We cannot let the variation (or lack) of definitions get in the way of gaining a fundamental understanding of the most basic element of the firm's operations and revenues. So, for now, we will put formal definitions aside and dive right into the data—warts and all—to make sense of it as a critical "health check" of the company's current and future prospects.

Having said that, we do not want to back away entirely from the main message of this chapter. While our analyses can proceed without a formal, fixed definition of the customer, they would surely be enhanced by the presence of one in any given analysis setting. Furthermore, the ability to take meaningful actions and to gauge their impact would be made stronger by a firm-wide understanding of who is (and is not) the customer.

Let us conclude this chapter with one more story to motivate the need to define (and count) a firm's customers. Several years ago, one of us (Pete) was working on a project with a major car rental firm. The goal was to help the firm, starting with its senior management team, to find and leverage new insights from its customer data. The Wharton researchers became frustrated by the firm's inability (not unwillingness—just pure inability) to answer what seemed to be the simplest of questions. At one point, a Wharton colleague said, "OK, let's start from the very beginning—how many unique customers do you have?" Silence. The executives all looked at each other, and no one could even formulate an educated guess.

Of course, the right answer should have been something like, "It depends on how you define a customer. Is it the person booking the trip, paying for it, driving the car, or perhaps the focal passenger?" But the executives could not formulate any kind of response at all.

The Wharton researcher quickly followed up with a seemingly similar question: "Well, how many cars do you have?" At that point several execs sprang to life, and enthusiastically reported a remarkably precise number—something like 432,400. That was too much for the CEO to handle. He pounded the table and said, "This is unacceptable! How can we know everything about our products and nothing about our customers?" It was an eye-opening moment for him—and thus for the rest of the team.

Many (if not most) companies continue to struggle with these issues; we hope that the frameworks and practices we lay out here will help shift them from "rule" to "exception" in the future.

Executive Questions

- How does your company define a customer? What are the criteria that underlie the definition, and how will that definition change as you engage in new business practices (e.g., new products/services or distribution channels)?
- If you are a public company, how is the term "customer" used and defined in your statutory reports, if at all?
- How consistent are you in your definition across business units and functional areas? Is there alignment across the organization regarding the definition (and measurement) of the customer?
- Are you guilty of casually throwing around statistics on the number of customers that reflect different business outcomes/objectives—but without being clear on what actually constitutes a customer?
- How does your ability to measure customers drive your definition of the customer (and vice versa)?

Chapter 2

The Data Cube and the Five Lenses

A business's "top line" (i.e., revenue) is simply the sum of the value of all the transactions that occurred in a given time period.

How can we describe each transaction? At the simplest level, we can describe it in terms of three characteristics: who made the purchase (customer), when it occurred (time), and what was purchased (product). Given these three characteristics, we can conceptualize the firm's transaction database as a cube of data, with the edges being customers, time, and products (figure 2.1).

Each unique product an individual customer purchases in a given transaction is represented by a non-zero-value cell in this cube. As only a few products are purchased by each customer in any given transaction, and as most customers do not buy every period, the overwhelming majority of the cells in the cube will contain zeroes.

Most organizations are structured around the products or services they provide; a product's success (or failure) in the marketplace is a very tangible indicator of a company's overall health. As such, most reporting systems are based on a view of the data cube in which only the product × time face is visible (figure 2.2). Summing over the customer dimension, we have a table where the rows are products and the columns are time.

The column totals computed from this data table are the firm's total revenue in each period. Focusing on a single row of the product × timetable allows us to examine a product's performance over

Figure 2.1. The Fundamental Data Cube

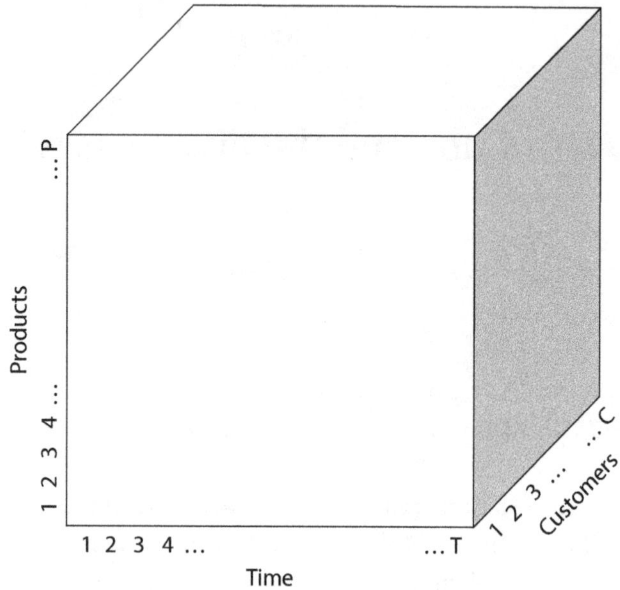

Figure 2.2. The Product × Time Face

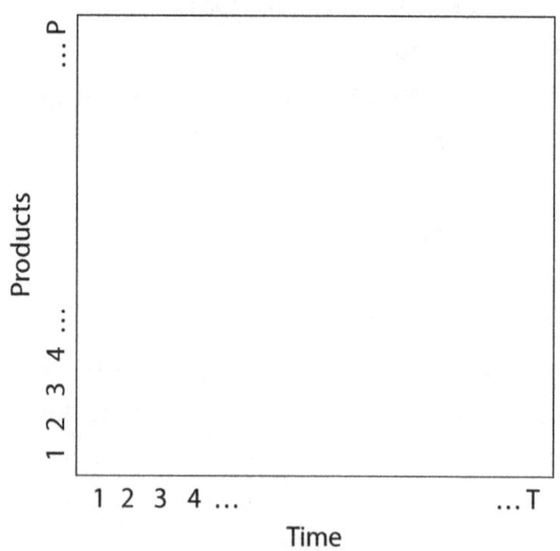

time. While we do not dismiss the value of reports generated from that particular 2D view of the data cube—after all, they are central to the day-to-day operations of most firms—they fail to give any insight into the behavior of the primary source of an organization's (inward) operating cash flow (its customers). If we wish to gain such insights, we need to view the cube from a different perspective.

We propose a conceptually simple change in perspective that can have a profound impact on the way your firm thinks about its business: Pivot the orientation of the data cube so the primary focus moves to the customer × time face (figure 2.3).

We are now aggregating over the product dimension. This seemingly simple shift in orientation opens up a whole new set of ways to think about your firm's revenues and profits.

Of course, for many firms, it is harder to get visibility of individual customers than it is to see/understand/measure each product, but that does not make the customer view any less important. Let us zoom in on this customer × time face and consider the stylized view given in figure 2.4. For now, assume that you can track the behavior of your firm's entire customer base from its first day of operations.

Figure 2.3. The Customer × Time Face

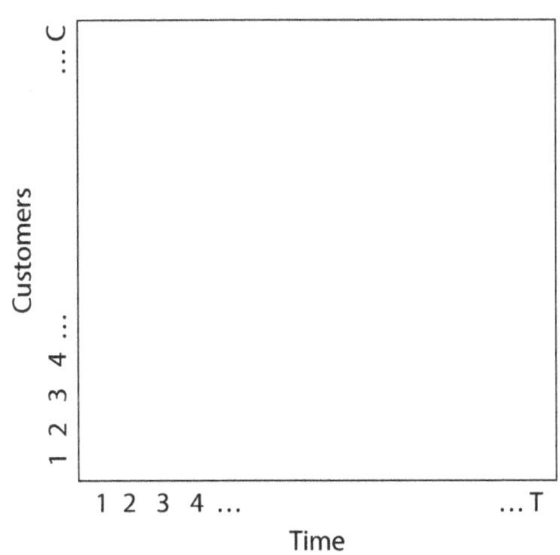

Figure 2.4. Customer Transactions over Time

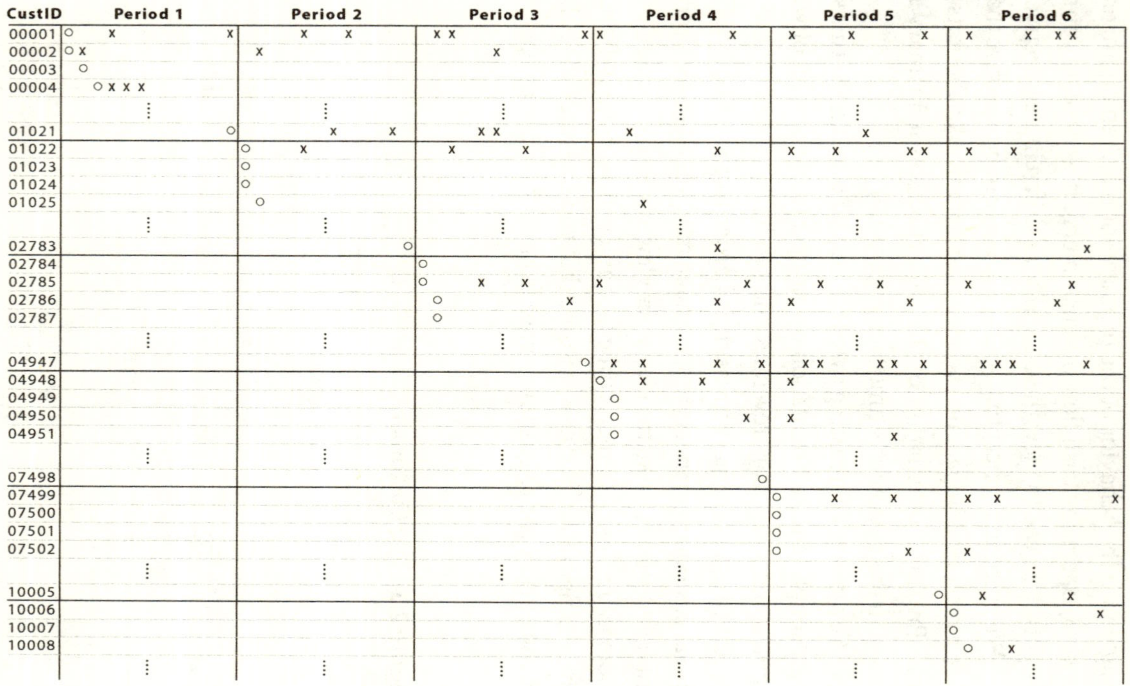

The occasion of a customer's first purchase from the firm is denoted by ○ and subsequent purchase occasions are denoted by ×s. (We assume that a customer is considered "acquired" when they make their first purchase from the firm. Some firms may have a different definition of acquisition, which we explore in chapter 9.) Each purchase occasion could be the purchase of one unit of one product or multiple units of multiple products. For now, we will ignore the product dimension and simply focus on the total value of the transaction (the product dimension will be reintroduced in chapter 8).

The rows are ordered by time of customer acquisition. Each row tracks the purchasing of a customer over time. Customers 00001–01021 were acquired in Period 1, customers 01022–02783 were acquired in Period 2, and so on. Some customers (e.g., 00003, 02787) make just one purchase and never make a repeat purchase, at least up to the end of Period 6. Others (e.g., 00002, 04948) make a few subsequent purchases before disappearing. And some customers (e.g., 00001, 04947) become frequent buyers.

Faced with such a view of the firm's customers' transaction histories, what types of analyses can we undertake? The core analyses we associate with a customer-base audit come from viewing this face through five different lenses.

The Five Lenses

The first lens focuses on a vertical slice of the customer × time face (figure 2.5). This allows us to explore the behavior of all the customers that made at least one transaction with the firm in the time period defined by the width of this slice, typically a quarter or a year. The basic analyses for a single time slice, which we explore in chapter 3, enable us to uncover the extent to which customers differ in their buying behavior and therefore value.

The second lens considers two adjacent vertical slices of the customer × time face (figure 2.6). Such a view of the data is triggered by different circumstances, such as a desire to evaluate the impact of a certain event (such as a natural disaster) or a failure to meet quarterly

Figure 2.5. Lens 1

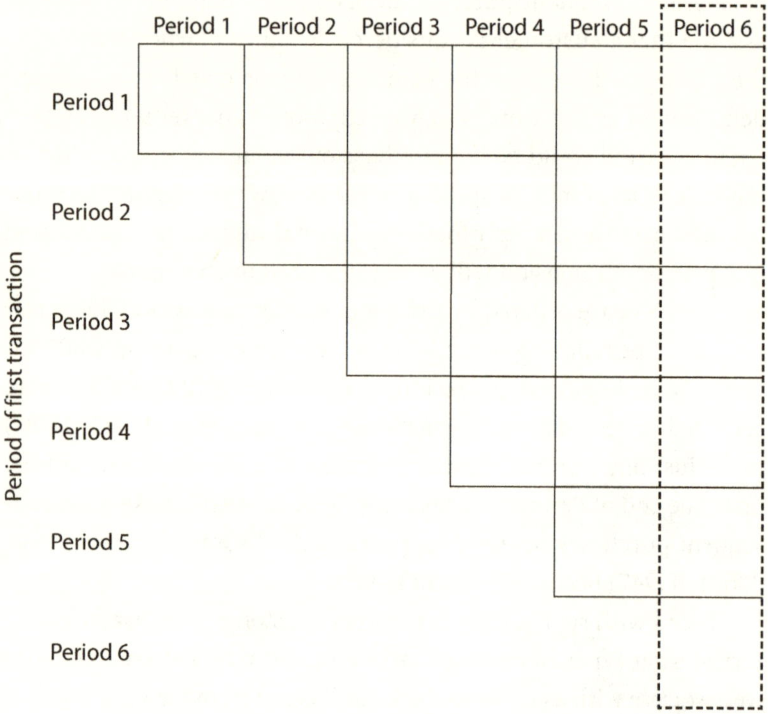

or annual revenue (and associated profit) targets. The basic analyses, which we explore in chapter 4, enable us to identify the changes in buyer behavior from one period to the next that underlie the period-on-period fluctuations in firm performance.

The third lens focuses on a horizontal slice of the customer × time face (figure 2.7). As such, we are exploring how the behavior of a *cohort* of customers evolves over time, starting from their first-ever transaction with the firm. (A "customer cohort" is defined as the set of customers acquired in the same time period—for example, those customers who make their first purchase in January, or the second quarter of the year.) The basic analyses, which we explore in chapter 5, enable us to identify the patterns of change—usually in the form of a decay—in buying behavior over time.

Figure 2.6. Lens 2

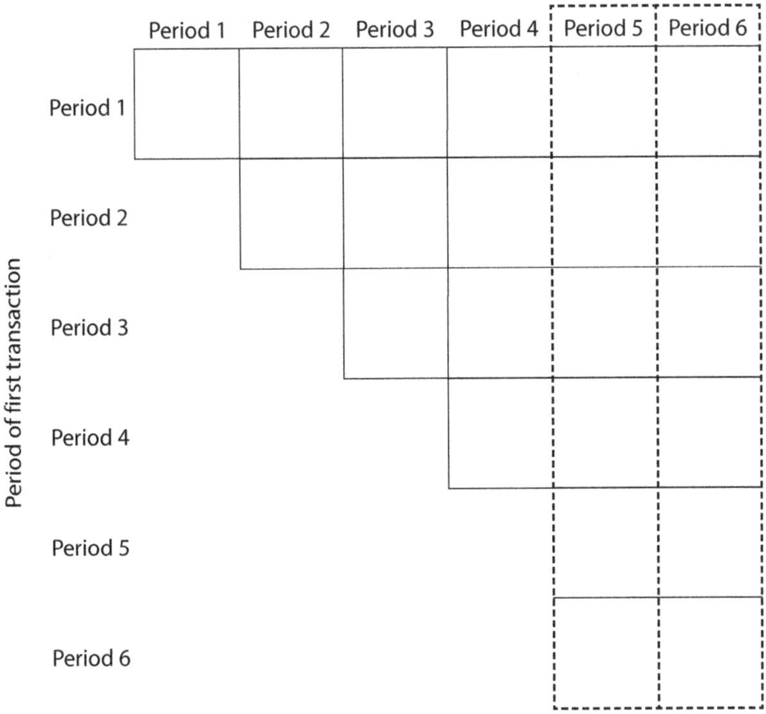

The third lens gets us thinking about the cohort as a unit of analysis. A natural next step is to ask how one cohort differs from another, which is the focus of the fourth lens (figure 2.8). In chapter 6, we explore the basic analyses that facilitate such a comparison.

Unlike Lens 2, which compares behaviors in one time period to another, Lens 4 compares groups of customers acquired in different periods of time. Like Lens 2, it can be motivated by internal or external changes that took place between the two periods. However, the way we evaluate those changes is not by looking at the immediate impact on revenue and profit, but instead by differences in the quality and quantity of customers acquired. This makes it a longer-term analysis, which can be a nice complement to the short-term view arising from Lens 2.

Figure 2.7. Lens 3

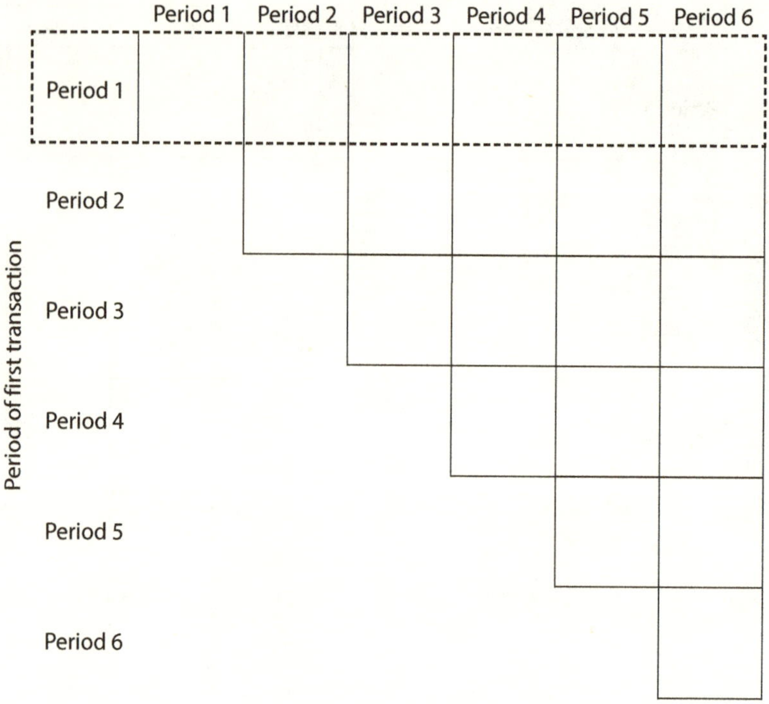

The fifth and final lens steps back and considers the whole customer × time face. As we explore in chapter 7, we draw on and integrate the types of analyses introduced via Lenses 1–4 to gain an overall customer-centric view of firm performance and to develop a sense of the health of our customer base (and therefore future revenue and profit streams).

The distinguishing characteristics of these five lenses are summarized in figure 2.9. Lens 1 is a single-period analysis, focusing on all those customers active in that period. Lens 2 is period versus period analysis, focusing on all those customers active in at least one of the two periods. Lens 3 is a single-cohort analysis, tracking over time the behavior of a group of customers "born" in the same time period. Lens 4 is a cohort versus cohort analysis, comparing and contrasting the evolution of buying behavior for two groups of custom-

Figure 2.8. Lens 4

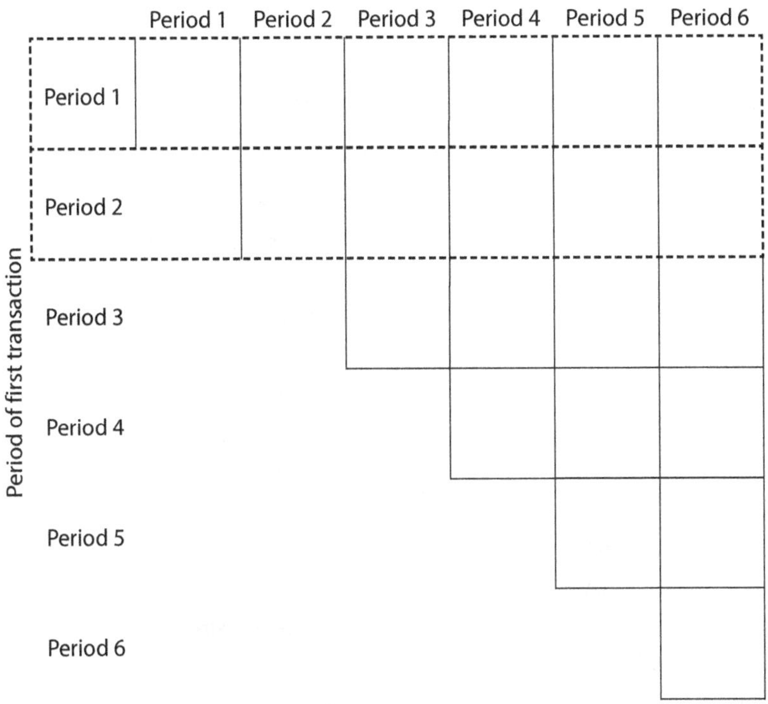

Figure 2.9. Classifying the Five Lenses

	Period	**Cohort**
One	Lens 1	Lens 3
Two	Lens 2	Lens 4
Three+	Lens 5	

ers "born" at different points. Lens 5 is a multiperiod analysis in which we focus on multiple cohorts.

Madrigal: Our Running Example

As we present the basic analyses associated with these five lenses (chapters 3–7) and then reintroduce the product dimension (chapter 8), we will use a dataset from a company we call Madrigal, Inc. This company is a US retailer with a strong 20-year catalog heritage that recently has accelerated its digitization with aggressive migration of customers to online channels. It has a small number of physical stores, but a popular loyalty program means the majority of its turnover is associated with known customers. The small percentage of anonymous transactions is ignored for the purposes of this analysis.

The starting point for defining a customer in this setting will be any named individual who has ever made a purchase from Madrigal. This will be further developed in each of the lenses.

We realize that most of the readers of this book will not be working in the retail sector. Should you continue reading? If you are in the business of selling nuclear reactors, probably not. Otherwise, yes. In our experience, when it comes to the types of analyses one can undertake to understand the behavior of a firm's customers, the differences between business settings are not as big as they may seem at first glance. This is true for all of the common frameworks used to describe businesses, such as B2B versus B2C, product versus service, high involvement versus low involvement products/services, and country/region of interest.

We have developed and fine-tuned the analyses we will discuss in many nonretail businesses. We encourage you to engage with this running example and then reflect on how the analyses might need to be adapted for your specific business setting. In chapter 9, we will broaden our scope to consider the key changes or additional analyses that may be required in other settings.

Our dataset covers the period 2016 to 2019. Figure 2.10 reports Madrigal's annual revenue and profit over this period. While 2017 was not a massive improvement over 2016, with only 7% growth in sales and 4% growth in profit, 2018 and 2019 were much better. For both years, revenues were up by 21%, and profits increased by 18% and 22%, respectively.

What exactly do we mean by revenue and profit? This is internal reporting, not financial reporting for external audiences. Revenue is simply the sum of each customer's total spend with the firm in the specified time period, net of any returned products. If someone purchases products priced at $100 with a 25% discount, this spend is recorded as $75. Similarly, profit is the sum of customer-level profit in the specified time period.

The measurement of customer-level profit is the Holy Grail for any firm that aspires to be customer centric. However, as you may

Figure 2.10. Summary of Madrigal's Annual Performance

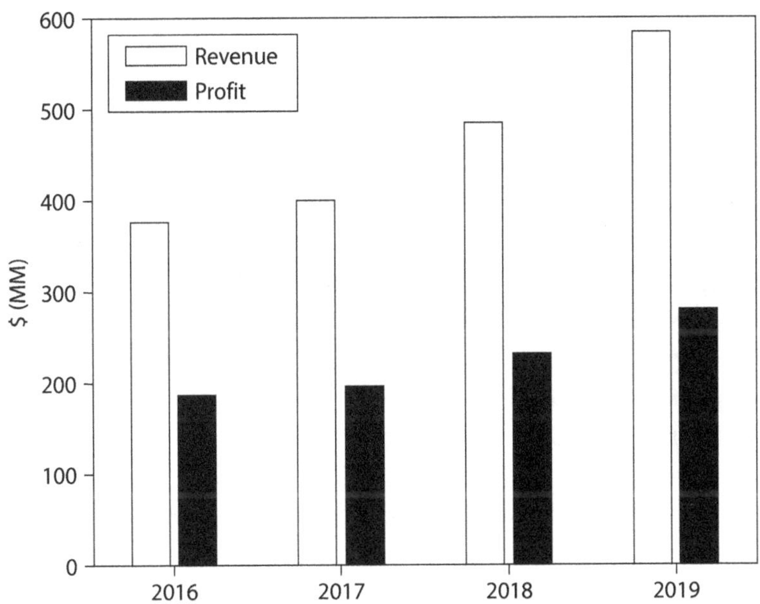

well know, identifying and allocating all the costs is a managerial accounting nightmare.

We can think of a spectrum of customer profitability measures. The simplest is spend minus direct product costs. The next step is to deduct both cost of goods and fully variable costs from spend. (For an online retailer, fully variable costs would typically include shipping costs, packaging, and credit card charges.) The final step would be to also deduct semi-variable costs, which for an online retailer would include operations such as picking, packing, and returns. In this running example, customer-level profit is simply spend minus direct product costs.

We view the measurement and analysis of customer profit as a journey. Right now, you may struggle to merge basic product costs with the sales data. But do not let that hold you back from performing the analyses we will discuss. Performing a customer-base audit using revenue alone is orders of magnitude better than not performing it at all. As your systems improve, you can shift the focus of your analyses to profit instead.

Digging Deeper into the Data

Before we start exploring the analyses associated with each lens, it is important that we have a basic understanding of the data used in any customer-base audit.

We started this chapter saying there are three key dimensions on which a transaction can be characterized: who made the purchase (customer), when it occurred (time), and what was purchased (product). While this is true, things get a little more complicated once we start getting into the details of the customer-base audit. Even if you do not have to deal with the details yourself, a (very) basic understanding is useful.

Somewhere in the depths of your operational IT systems will be a database in which the basic details of each transaction will be recorded. The table will look something like the extract reported in table 2.1. Each row corresponds to one line of an itemized receipt or

Table 2.1. Raw Transaction Data

Order_ID	Customer_ID	Date	SKU_ID	Quantity	Price
1102615	0154253	2019-10-03	25915	1	5.00
1102615	0154253	2019-10-03	29747	4	39.90
1102615	0154253	2019-10-03	2541	4	59.90
1102615	0154253	2019-10-03	45835	2	149.00
1102616	0034679	2019-10-03	3800	1	199.00
1102617	1158577	2019-10-03	3385	1	29.50
1102617	1158577	2019-10-03	3384	1	10.00
1102617	1158577	2019-10-03	2640	1	10.00
1102617	1158577	2019-10-03	3386	1	5.00
1102617	1158577	2019-10-03	2250	1	19.50

invoice. Note that very little information is recorded. In this example, which shows the details of three consecutive transactions, we have a unique ID assigned to each transaction, the ID number of the customer making the transaction, the code associated with each SKU (stock-keeping unit) purchased, the quantity of each unit purchased, and the price per unit.

We see that customer 1158577 purchased five different products in the one order they placed on October 3. What were these products? Through what channel did they make the purchase? What was the payment method? Who is this customer? Such information is not recorded here.

Elsewhere in your firm's IT systems will be a customer file that contains all the basic information about each customer (e.g., name, address, email address, phone number). There will also be a product file that contains a complete description of each SKU in a very detailed manner (e.g., brand, size, color). There will be an order file that tells us other things about each order (e.g., channel, online browser if applicable, payment method). At some stage it will be necessary to merge these files with the raw transaction data file, but that is not something you need to worry about.

However, you should not assume it is costless. Your firm may have made major investments in systems that have effectively merged the data and make it very easy to query it. If not, the process of blending the data from these various sources, which is referred to as ETL (extract, transform, load), can be a time-consuming process.

This raw transaction data is of limited use by itself for the core analyses presented in this book. The first thing we need to do is to aggregate it to the order level. That is, we sum over all the rows associated with each order ID, resulting in a table that contains one row per order. Referring back to table 2.1, customer 0154253 purchased four unique SKUs, buying one unit of SKU 25915, four units of SKUs 29747 and 02541, and two units of SKU 45835. Multiplying the quantity times the price and summing up gives us a total spend of $702.20. In this case, margin information is available (via other data tables), so we can compute the profit associated with each order. This results in a basic order-level summary of buying behavior as illustrated in table 2.2.

Table 2.2. Transaction-Level Summary of Buying Behavior

Order_ID	Customer_ID	Date	Spend	Profit
1102612	2164322	2019-10-02	560.00	195.79
1102613	0035135	2019-10-02	430.00	141.76
1102614	0070471	2019-10-03	1848.80	641.97
1102615	0154253	2019-10-03	702.20	364.15
1102616	0034679	2019-10-03	199.00	112.73
1102617	0158577	2019-10-03	74.00	45.46
1102618	0279314	2019-10-03	180.00	37.98
1102619	0924751	2019-10-03	448.00	239.05
1102620	0000476	2019-10-03	220.00	64.96
1102621	0031888	2019-10-03	1651.90	898.72

A dataset with this basic structure is the dataset on which all the analyses associated with Lenses 1–5 will be based.

For many of the analyses, we can go one step further, aggregating individual transactions by customer ID for each given period (e.g., quarter, year). This results in a table where each row summarizes the behavior of each customer in each period. Table 2.3 reports such a summary when each customer's transactions are aggregated to the annual level. We see that customer 0154253 made a total of three purchases in 2019. Their total spend was $1,931.11 and they contributed $843.23 in profit.

A dataset with this basic structure provides the basis for all the analyses associated with Lenses 1 and 2. If an individual's transactions are aggregated to the quarterly level (as opposed to the annual level), such a table is enough for most of the Lens 1–5 analyses. Despite the costs/complexities noted above, it is a reasonable expectation that all companies should have the capability to create such a dataset—or are making high-priority investments to develop such a capability.

Table 2.3. Customer-Level Summary of Annual Buying Behavior

Customer_ID	Year	Num_trans	Tot_spend	Tot_profit
0154253	2019	3	1931.11	843.23
0154331	2019	2	319.00	195.31
0154985	2019	1	100.00	47.36
0156053	2019	1	50.00	15.42
0157546	2019	7	1249.00	306.59
0158577	2019	4	494.10	165.23
0158745	2019	2	190.00	22.54
0159744	2019	1	199.00	66.17
0160711	2019	8	3402.50	1754.50
0170100	2019	3	277.90	159.39

Conclusion

Any kind of audit—whether focusing on customers, overall firm finances, or those conducted in nonbusiness domains (e.g., a clinical audit in a medical setting)—begins with data. And the collection/assembly of a dataset begins with a clear understanding of how that data can (and should) be viewed.

This is why we emphasize the importance of the "data cube" before beginning any analyses. A transaction database can be quite complex, so this metaphor can be a useful way to bring some structure and priority to the different ways of looking at data. For the purposes of a customer-base audit, one side of the cube merits the highest priority: the customer × time face.

Even when we limit our scope to this one viewpoint, there is still some complexity to be managed; this is where the five lenses come in. None of them should come as a total surprise to the reader, but understanding the relationship between them and, ultimately, the kinds of decisions that will arise from each one will be the focus of our work in the pages to come.

Let the customer-base audit begin!

Executive Questions

- Does the data cube reflect the kinds of conversations and analyses (e.g., product × time, customer × time) that take place for your firm?
- What will it take to shift most of those conversations from focusing on the product × time face to the customer × time face?
- How do you tie this fundamental understanding of data structures to the way that decisions are made and evaluated?
- Can you produce the kinds of transaction tables as shown for Madrigal? If not, what are the main hurdles you will need to overcome?

- How does your firm view the IT expenditures required to perform such tasks—are they seen as costs or investments?
- How do you allocate fixed and variable costs to each transaction and to each customer? Are there formal written guidelines, and do you handle these issues consistently across your firm?

Chapter 3

How Different Are Your Customers?

You most certainly know last year's revenue and profit numbers. But what do you know about the behavior of the pool of customers that lies behind these numbers? For example:

- How many customers (whether consumers or businesses) made at least one purchase from you last year?
- What percentage of these customers made only one purchase?
- How reliant are you on a small group of customers? For example, how many customers accounted for half of your revenue? For half of your profit?
- What percentage of your customers was unprofitable?

These questions, and more, are answered by the set of Lens 1 analyses presented in this chapter, all of which summarize some aspect of customer buying behavior in a single time period (e.g., year).

The Foundational Plots

Madrigal's revenue for 2019 was $583 million, with an associated profit of $280 million. Defining a customer as anyone who purchased from the firm in 2019, Madrigal had 3.2 million customers (3,185,335 to be exact) that year. The average spend per 2019 customer was therefore

$183. But did these customers differ that much in terms of their total spend with Madrigal in 2019?

The total 2019 spend of individual customers ranged from $0.01 to $40,149. In order to visualize the distribution of spend across customers, we create "spend bins" that are $25 wide, with a final bin for more than $1,000, and count the number of customers whose total spend in 2019 fell into each bin. A plot of the resulting frequency distribution is given in figure 3.1; the left y-axis reports the relative frequency (i.e., the percentage of customers that fell into each bin), while the right y-axis reports the raw number of customers associated with each bin.

Looking at the height of the left-most bar, we see that 7% of the customers (221,000 individuals) spent between $0 and $25 with the firm in 2019. Looking at the height of the second bar, we see that 14% (456,000 individuals) spent between $25 and $50. And so on. Looking at the right-most bar, we see that over 1% of the customers (45,000 individuals) spent more than $1,000 with the firm in 2019.

Figure 3.1. Distribution of Total Spend Across All Individuals Making at Least One Purchase in 2019

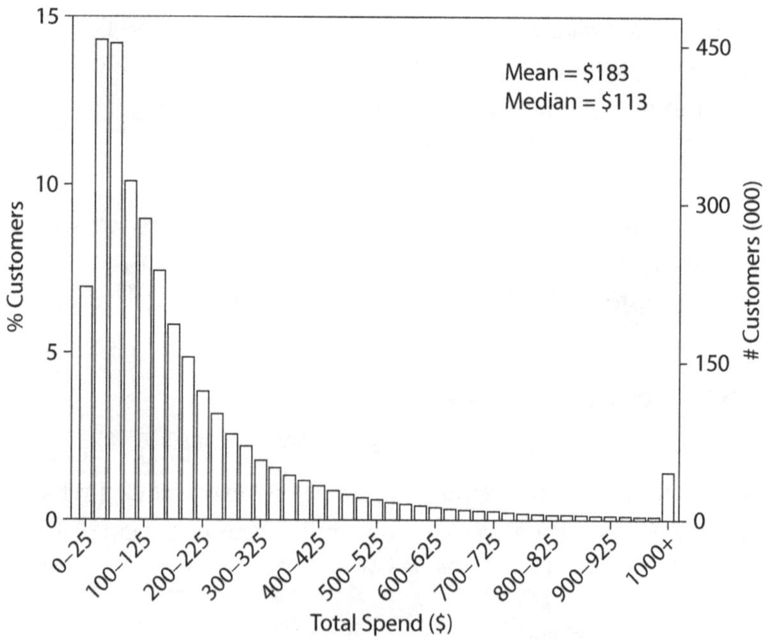

This distribution of total spend is what statisticians call a right-skewed distribution: While most of the observations (in this case, customers) are located to the left of the figure, the right tail is very drawn out (extending, in this case, to $40,149). We note that, as is typically the case for right-skewed distributions, the mean is higher than the median. Half of Madrigal's 2019 customers spent less than $113 in total (the definition of the median); just over 69% of the customers spent less than the average total spend per customer of $183.

An immediate takeaway is that any discussion of "the average customer" is misleading, and such a phrase should be purged from your vocabulary. It is very clear that customers differ greatly in their value.

Since we know the number of transactions made by each customer, further insight into how customers differ can be gained by applying the following multiplicative decomposition of each customer's total spend:

$$\begin{aligned}\text{total spend} &= \#\ \text{transactions} \times \frac{\text{total spend}}{\#\ \text{transactions}} \\ &= \#\ \text{transactions} \times \text{average spend per transaction}\end{aligned}$$

Then, we look at how the two quantities vary across customers. Let us first consider the variation in transactions. Madrigal's 3.2 million customers made a total of nearly 6.1 million transactions that year. The average number of transactions per customer was therefore 1.9. By definition, all customers had to have made at least one purchase that year. One customer made a total of 201 transactions.

To visualize the distribution of the number of transactions across customers, we count how many people made just one transaction in 2019, how many people made two, and so on up to 10 or more. The resulting frequency distribution is plotted in figure 3.2.

Looking at the height of the first bar, we see that 63% of the customers made only one transaction with Madrigal in 2019. Looking at the height of the second bar, we see that 18% of customers made only two transactions. In other words, 81% of the customers made just

Figure 3.2. Distribution of the Number of Transactions Made by Customers in 2019

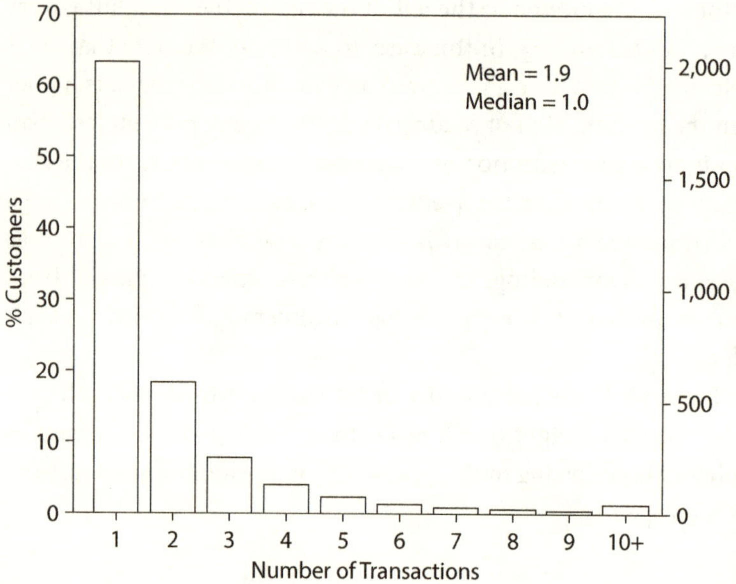

one or two transactions in the year. Looking at the right-hand side of this plot, we see that just over 1% of customers made 10 or more transactions with the firm.

As with the distribution of total spend, this distribution is highly right-skewed. Once again, this means that the average number of transactions is not the most meaningful summary of customer behavior.

Does this mean the skewed nature of the distribution of total spend across customers is driven purely by the skewed nature of the distribution of the number of transactions? To answer this question, let us also consider the distribution of average spend per transaction across all 3.2 million customers.

We first compute each customer's average spend per transaction (which ranges from $0.01 to $14,500) and then count the number of people falling into bins of width $25 (with a greater-than-$500 bin). This frequency distribution is plotted in figure 3.3.

Figure 3.3. Distribution of Average Spend per Transaction

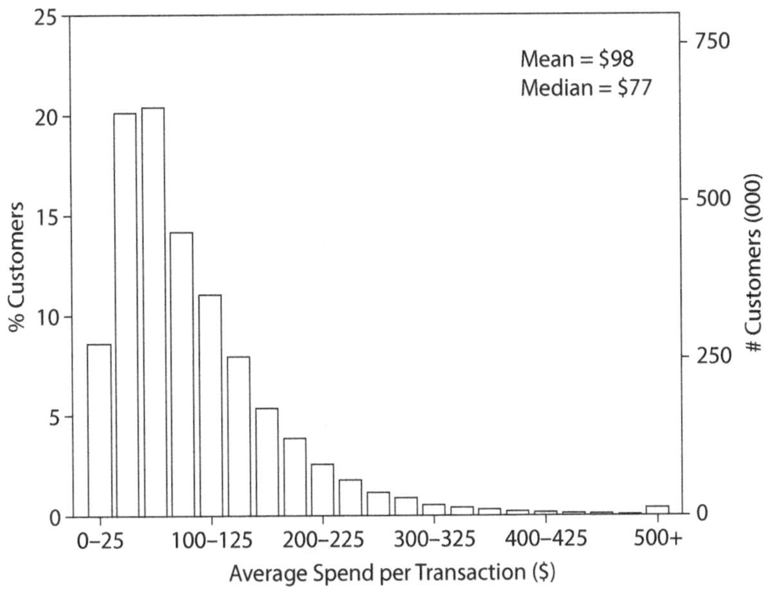

Once again, the distribution is right-skewed. Half the customers had an average spend per transaction of less than $77. Just over 62% of the customers had an average spend per transaction less than the average across all 2019 customers of $98. So, no: The skewed nature of the distribution of total spend across customers is not driven only by the skewed nature of the distribution of the number of transactions. It also reflects the skewed nature of the distribution of average spend per customer. Each of these behaviors, by itself, reflects an interesting and important spread across customers that should be carefully tracked and understood by any organization.

An important statistical aside: If you have an extra-good memory for numbers, you will remember the average total spend per customer was $183, and the average number of transactions per customer was 1.9. Doesn't this imply the mean average spend per transaction should be $183/1.9 = $96? Why do we see a mean of $98 instead?

To help understand this, consider the following toy example. A firm has two customers in a given year. Customer A makes one transaction, spending \$50. Customer B makes two transactions, spending \$35 on the first transaction and \$45 on the second. The firm's total revenue is \$130, which means the average total spend per customer is \$65. The total number of transactions is three, which means the average number of transactions per customer is 1.5. The average spend per transaction for customer A is \$50 and \$40 for customer B. The mean average spend per transaction is therefore \$45. This is equivalent to the \$98 reported above. The equivalent of the \$96 number considered above is $\$65/1.5 = \$43$. If we weight each customer's average spend per transaction by their share of transactions, we have $1/3 \times \$50 + 2/3 \times \$40 = \$43$. And we also get the same answer if we divide the total revenue by the total number of transactions: $\$130/3 = \$43$.

In other words, \$98 is the unweighted-mean average spend per transaction, in which each customer is given equal weight, and \$96 is the weighted-mean average, which depends on the number of transactions each customer made. Averages of averages can be confusing. It is important that you understand exactly what is being reported when you see such numbers.

Given the variability in both the number of transactions and average spend per transaction across customers, it is natural to ask whether these two quantities are related. Some people think they would be positively correlated: People who buy frequently really like the firm and spend a lot per transaction. Others think the two quantities should be negatively correlated: Customers have a fixed budget, and some choose to spend it all at once, while others spread it over a number of transactions, resulting in a smaller average spend per transaction.

Rather than discussing this on a purely conceptual basis, let us focus on the data. For this dataset, the correlation between the number of transactions and average spend per transaction is −0.03. Given the number of observations, this is statistically significant, but practically speaking we can treat these two quantities as if they are independent.

Digging a bit deeper, table 3.1 reports the median and mean spend per transaction separately. While there is some variability in both the median and mean spend per transaction as the number of transactions customers made increases, there is no strong relationship between these two quantities, at least for Madrigal.

Turning our attention to profitability, recall that Madrigal's 3.2 million 2019 customers generated a profit of $280 million, an average profit of $88 per customer. However, the profitability of individual customers in 2019 ranged from a loss of $2,470 to a profit of $22,139.

To visualize the differences in customer profitability, we bin the data in the following manner. For customers whose profit was between $0 and $500 (98% of the 2019 customer base), we count how many individuals fall into $25-wide bins. We also have a bin for those customers on which the firm made a loss (just under 1% of all 2019 customers) and a bin for those whose profit in 2019 was above $500. This frequency distribution is plotted in figure 3.4.

Once again, we see a right-skewed distribution. It turns out that 69% of Madrigal's 2019 customers had a profit below the overall average of $88.

Another way of looking at the profitability of each customer is to consider their average margin, which we define as their profit divided by total spend. For customers that were profitable, we count how many fall into margin bins that are 5% wide and plot the numbers in figure 3.5, along with a bin for those customers on which the firm made a loss and therefore had a negative margin.

Table 3.1. Median and Mean Spend per Transaction by Transaction Level

	Number of Transactions									
	1	2	3	4	5	6	7	8	9	10+
Median	$72	$81	$82	$82	$81	$80	$79	$78	$77	$76
Mean	$99	$99	$98	$95	$94	$91	$90	$89	$88	$86

Figure 3.4. Distribution of Customer Profit in 2019

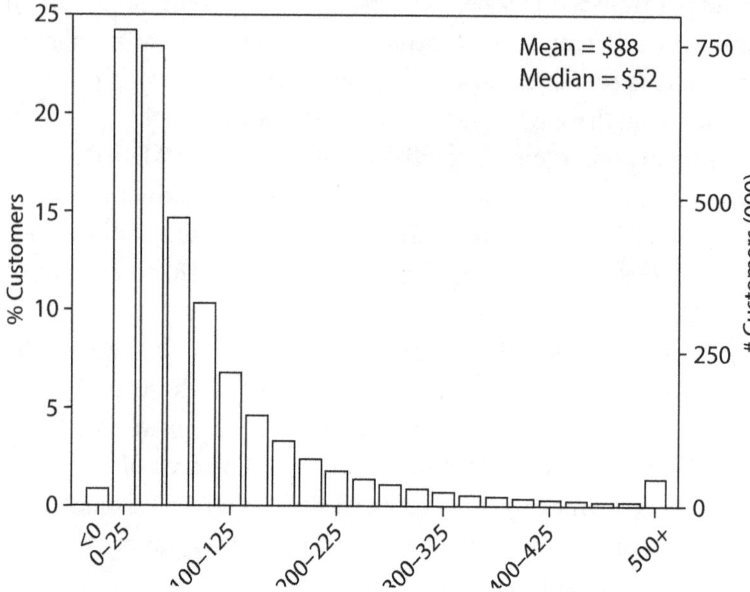

Figure 3.5. Distribution of Average Margin in 2019

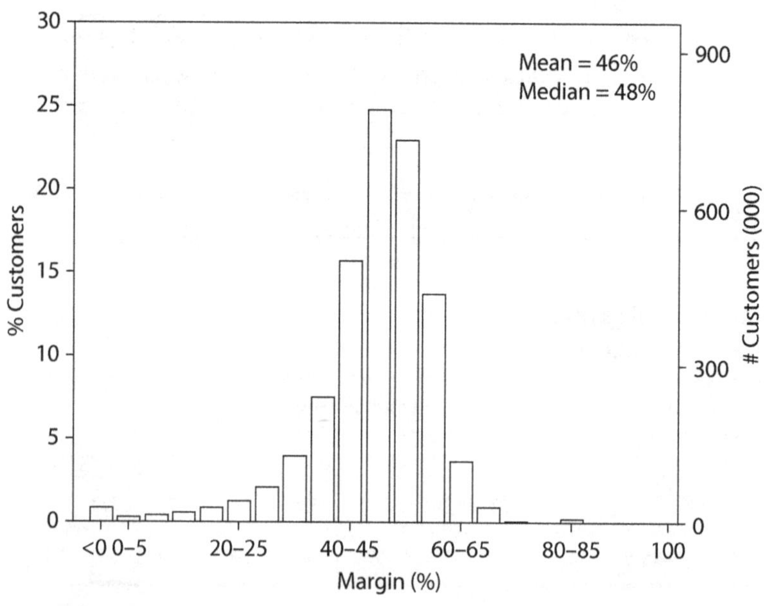

The distribution of margin is much less skewed than that of the other quantities considered above. The mean and median are very similar. Summing the heights of the four highest bars, we see that 77% of the customers had an average margin between 40% and 60%.

What distinguishes those customers with low profit margins? Recall that, for the case of Madrigal, we are defining customer-level profit as spend minus direct product costs. Therefore, a customer who has a lower average margin is most likely buying a lot of lower-margin products at their regular price or is "cherry-picking" (heavily) discounted products when such promotions become available.

We noted in the last chapter that we can think of a spectrum of customer profitability measures. Depending on how we measure and allocate costs, we can further deduct fully variable costs such as shipping, packaging, and credit card charges and then semi-variable costs such as picking, packing, and returns handling. As we refine our measure of customer profitability, we can expect the distribution of average margin to become a lot more left-skewed.

Can You Generalize These Patterns?

We have seen these kinds of patterns across hundreds of different companies. The distributions of the total spend, number of transactions, average spend per transaction, and profit are almost always highly skewed, just as observed here. Most people make few purchases with the company—in almost all cases, the modal number is one—and as a result, their overall spend with the firm is small. However, there are some customers who make a large number of purchases and spend a lot with the firm.

Just how skewed the distribution is depends on the context. For example, in B2C settings, the consumption of "vice" products (e.g., alcohol and tobacco) can be very skewed, with a small number of customers buying and consuming very large amounts of the product. Similarly, the consumption of online products (e.g., gaming) tends to be very skewed, with there being a small number of *very* heavy users.

In B2B settings, we can also see extremely skewed distributions, with the differences in customer-level demand reflecting the different sizes of the customers. For example, if you sell office supplies, you would expect a customer with 20,000 employees to purchase more than a small mom-and-pop store. As such, in some B2B settings, it may make sense to first segment the customer base by number of employees or total revenue (e.g., small and medium-sized businesses, "mid-market" and large enterprises) and then perform the analyses separately for each segment.

Sometimes the distributions will not be so smooth, but there will typically be a logical explanation. For example, when analyzing the distribution of spend for a major London theater, we found that while the general shape of spend per customer was right-skewed, it was quite spiky. There are two obvious factors at work. First, the price of seats can vary greatly depending on where you sit in the theater. On average, the most expensive seats were more than 15 times more expensive than the cheapest seats. Second, if we look at the number of tickets purchased per performance, it is more likely that two tickets were purchased than just one. Similarly, it was more common to see four tickets being purchased rather than three. Thus, even the distribution of spend for those customers buying tickets for just one performance in a year was very spiky. Another such example is donations to a major public radio station in the Midwest region of the United States. The "spend" distribution was mostly defined by the specific donation amounts tied to different premium offerings (e.g., umbrellas, tote bags), and these target amounts would vary from year to year.

The Vital Few and the Useful Many

For anyone undertaking a customer-base audit for the first time, the plots we have just considered comprise the fundamental starting point. Too many executives do not understand the level of variability in buying behavior and value across their firm's customer base.

Even more important, they do not appreciate just how skewed these distributions are. Recall that just over 69% of customers spent less than the average customer and had a profit less than that of the average consumer. It should be clear that it is very misleading to talk about "the average customer." Such a person is not representative of your "typical" customer (to the extent that there is such a thing as a "typical" customer at all).

The fact that the majority of customers are below that average means there exists a small number of customers who account for a sizable chunk of the firm's revenues and profits. Not all customers are equal in their value to the firm; a lot of the value is concentrated in a small subset of them.

A useful way of communicating this is via a decile analysis. As the name suggests, this sees us dividing the customer base into 10 equally sized groups and then summarizing the behavior of these groups. We will consider two versions of this.

For our first decile analysis, we sort the 2019 customers on the basis of their 2019 profitability, from most profitable to least profitable. The first decile comprises the most profitable 10% of customers, the second decile comprises the next most profitable 10% of customers, down to the tenth decile, which comprises the least profitable 10% of customers. We report in table 3.2 the number of customers in each decile, the total number of transactions made by these customers, and the associated revenue and profit. These decile quantities are then expressed as a percentage of the totals for the firm.

Reading across the first row, we see that the top 10% of customers (decile 1) accounted for 40% of Madrigal's profits in 2019. Almost 60% (58%, to be exact) of the firm's profit came from just 20% of its customers (deciles 1 and 2). At the other end, the bottom 10% of customers (decile 10) accounted for just 1% of Madrigal's profit.

To get some insight into the differences between deciles, we find it useful to employ the following multiplicative decomposition of the profit associated with each decile.

Table 3.2. Summary of 2019 Buyer Behavior by Customer Decile

Decile	Customers (000)	Transactions (000)	Revenue ($MM)	Profit ($MM)	% Cust	% Trans	% Rev	% Profit
1	319	1,653	$226	$112	10%	27%	39%	40%
2	319	851	$100	$49	10%	14%	17%	18%
3	319	642	$69	$34	10%	11%	12%	12%
4	319	534	$52	$25	10%	9%	9%	9%
5	319	488	$41	$19	10%	8%	7%	7%
6	319	441	$31	$14	10%	7%	5%	5%
7	319	402	$24	$11	10%	7%	4%	4%
8	319	374	$18	$8	10%	6%	3%	3%
9	319	358	$13	$5	10%	6%	2%	2%
10	319	350	$9	$2	10%	6%	2%	1%
	3,185	6,093	$583	$280				

As a first step, we decompose the total profit associated with each decile in the following manner:

$$\begin{aligned}\text{profit} &= \#\text{customers} \times \frac{\text{profit}}{\#\text{customers}} \\ &= \#\text{customers} \times \text{average profit per customer}\end{aligned}$$

Next, to get a sense of what lies behind any observed differences in average profit per customer, we use the following multiplicative decomposition:

$$\begin{aligned}&\text{average profit per customer} \\ &\quad = \frac{\text{profit}}{\#\text{customers}} \\ &\quad = \frac{\text{revenue}}{\#\text{customers}} \times \frac{\text{profit}}{\text{revenue}} \\ &\quad = \text{average spend per customer} \times \text{average margin}\end{aligned}$$

Finally, to get a sense of what lies behind any observed differences in average spend per customer, we decompose it in the following manner:

$$\begin{aligned}&\text{average spend per customer} \\ &\quad = \frac{\text{revenue}}{\#\text{customers}} \\ &\quad = \frac{\#\text{transactions}}{\#\text{customers}} \times \frac{\text{revenue}}{\#\text{transactions}} \\ &\quad = \begin{matrix}\text{average order} \\ \text{frequency (AOF)}\end{matrix} \times \begin{matrix}\text{average order} \\ \text{value(AOV)}\end{matrix}\end{aligned}$$

These three decompositions are summarized in figure 3.6.

Applying this to the data in table 3.2 gives us the decomposition of decile value reported in table 3.3. (Note that AOF × AOV × average margin = average profit per customer.)

Figure 3.6. A Multiplicative Decomposition of Profit

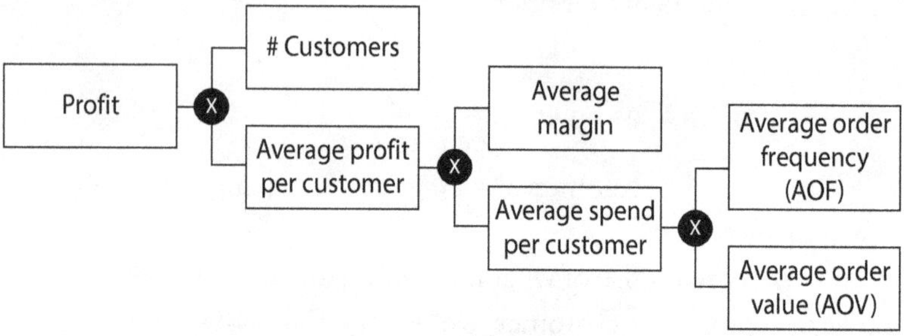

Table 3.3. Decomposition of Customer-Decile Profit

Decile	% Customers	% Profit	Avg spend per cust	Avg profit per cust	AOF	AOV	Avg Margin
1	10%	40%	$710	$353	5.2	$137	50%
2	10%	18%	$312	$154	2.7	$117	49%
3	10%	12%	$216	$106	2.0	$107	49%
4	10%	9%	$164	$79	1.7	$98	48%
5	10%	7%	$128	$60	1.5	$83	47%
6	10%	5%	$99	$45	1.4	$71	46%
7	10%	4%	$76	$34	1.3	$60	45%
8	10%	3%	$57	$25	1.2	$49	43%
9	10%	2%	$41	$17	1.1	$37	40%
10	10%	1%	$29	$6	1.1	$27	21%
			$183	$88	1.9	$96	48%

The general pattern we observe is that the higher-value deciles are more profitable because of higher overall spend rather than average margin. What lies behind their spend pattern? They have more transactions with the firm (AOF), and they spend more on each transaction (AOV). For example, comparing the top two deciles, while there is a small difference in average margin, the major driver of the difference in average profitability is the fact they have more transactions with the firm; the AOF for decile 1 is 93% higher than that for decile 2 ((5.2–2.7)/2.7 = 0.93). The difference in spend per transaction is much lower; the AOV for decile 1 is 17% higher than that for decile 2 ((137–117)/117 = 0.17).

For lower-value deciles, the key driver of differences in decile value is the differences in AOV, as well as the lower margins observed for the lowest decile, likely characterized by a disproportionate amount of light-buying "cherry pickers."

Can we get a deeper sense as to what lies behind the variation in AOF and AOV? We will set this important question aside for now, but we will explore it in chapter 8, when we "bring back" the product dimension of the fundamental data cube.

Recall from our discussion of the distribution of customer-level profit (figure 3.4) that Madrigal made a loss on just under 1% of its customers. These customers are included in decile 10. Some people like to pull out the loss-making customers and perform a separate analysis on them. The multiplicative decomposition of the losses associated with these customers is AOF = 1.4, AOV = $44, and average margin = –19%.

An alternative approach to performing a decile analysis is to create deciles that contain groups that each account for 10% of the firm's overall profit, as opposed to each decile containing 10% of the customers. (Which way you choose to create the deciles is largely a matter of taste, potentially influenced by the "story" you want to tell the audience.) We report this alternative summary in table 3.4.

What jumps out at us is the fact that the top 1% of Madrigal's customers (decile 1) are as profitable as the bottom 41% (decile 10). This does not mean that this latter set of customers should be "fired"; after all, they are still worth 10% of Madrigal's profit. Looking beyond these two deciles, we note that half of the firm's 2019 profits came from 15% of the customers (deciles 1 to 5). These observations should trigger further investigation into the characteristics of these customer groups and a discussion of how to manage them.

Table 3.4. Summary of Profit Deciles

Decile	% Customers	% Profit	Avg spend per cust	Avg profit per cust	AOF	AOV	Avg Margin
1	1%	10%	$1,700	$843	10.9	$156	50%
2	2%	10%	$869	$433	6.3	$138	50%
3	3%	10%	$602	$300	4.6	$132	50%
4	4%	10%	$450	$223	3.6	$125	50%
5	5%	10%	$347	$171	2.9	$119	49%
6	7%	10%	$269	$132	2.4	$113	49%
7	9%	10%	$209	$102	2.0	$106	49%
8	11%	10%	$160	$77	1.7	$96	48%
9	17%	10%	$112	$52	1.5	$77	47%
10	41%	10%	$52	$21	1.2	$45	41%
			$183	$88	1.9	$96	48%

Conclusion

The Lens 1 analyses presented in this chapter are not only a good first step in a customer-base audit, but they reveal important insights that are no less critical than those that will arise in the deeper, more complex analyses to follow. Specifically, the Lens 1 views encourage us to "celebrate heterogeneity," in other words, to see and acknowledge the existence of the small but powerful set of customers who buy more frequently, at greater average order values, and at (slightly) higher margins than the vast majority of the customer base. Companies that ignore these differences across their customers do so at great risk. Alternatively, those that are able to recognize and act on these differences are sowing the seeds for an effective and sustainable growth strategy.

We have mentioned it several times now, but we cannot say it enough: *There is no average customer.* But this does not mean the customer base is chaotic and unpredictable; quite the contrary, the key figures above reflect a lot of consistency about the nature of cross-customer variation within a given period. These sources of variation can be anticipated and leveraged effectively, rather than naively treating every customer the same, or by overcomplicating the customer relationship management task by going too far with well-intended but hard to implement "1:1 marketing" tactics.

An effective summary of Lens 1—and the lenses to follow—can be expressed as the "three Ds" of analyzing customer behavior: distribution, decomposition, and decile.

- We are used to seeing averages, but they can be misleading. It is important that we understand the true nature of the variation in customer behavior, and this comes from looking at **distributions**.
- We are used to seeing totals, but we gain insight by decomposing these totals into their constituent parts, be it an additive or multiplicative **decomposition**.
- We are used to making statements about the nature of behavior across our entire customer base, that is, making the implicit assumption that the "drivers" of behavior are the same for everyone. But the **decile** analyses (whether doing so on the basis of equal-sized groups of customers or equal-sized portions of customer profitability) show that this is not at all true. It is vitally important to understand how and why the top-decile customers are different from the lower ones.

What we have seen here for Madrigal is quite typical of the patterns that exist for most companies. As you begin your own customer-base audit, you should expect to see them as well. Of course, this is not a guarantee, but by having these patterns in mind as a reference point, you will be better able to identify and then, hopefully, to explain differences that might arise from time to time, or on a systematic basis.

Executive Questions

- How easily can you access the various figures and tables highlighted here? Must they be created as a custom exercise by a specialized analyst, or can the executive team easily access them "on-demand"?
- How do your Lens 1 views compare to those shown here? Do you see the same basic patterns for most of them (such as right-skewed distributions)?
- What kinds of specific deviations arise, and can you explain them? Do you believe that these differences are enduring characteristics of your customer base, or perhaps transient variations?
- Can your firm easily perform the multiplicative profit decomposition described above? If not, where are the bottlenecks in your reporting systems?
- As you start to isolate the best (top decile) customers, do you have any sense of how they differ from your other customers (beyond their greater purchasing and profitability)?
- What about the bottom-decile customers? Are you aware of their characteristics, and possible ways to bolster their profitability (e.g., by mitigating their cherry-picking behavior)?

Chapter 4

What Changed Since Last Period?

You have just received last year's results, and you are comparing your firm's performance to that of the previous year. Regardless of whether you met your targets, how do you approach this exercise?

If we view the customer as the fundamental unit of analysis, what questions do we ask to understand what lies behind the change in overall performance? To what extent does it simply reflect a change in the number of customers (defined, in this case, as anyone who purchased from the firm in the given year)? Focusing on customer-level behavior, was there much of a change in the number of transactions per customer? Did customers change in terms of their average spend per transaction? Their margins? These questions, and others, can be answered by a set of Lens 2 analyses, which summarize how customer behavior changed from one period to the next.

Initial Analysis

Madrigal's revenue for 2019 was $583 million, with an associated profit of $280 million. These numbers represent a 21% and 22% increase, respectively, over Madrigal's 2018 revenue of $483 million and profit of $230 million. What changes in customer behavior lie behind these increases?

A natural starting point would be to conduct a Lens 1 analysis for 2018 and see how the patterns of behavior changed from year to year. We know from the last chapter that Madrigal had nearly

3.2 million customers in 2019. In 2018, it had a little more than 2.6 million customers. In figure 4.1, we report the four basic distributions that were covered in the previous chapter. While the raw number of customers in each bin will have increased because we have more customers in 2019 than in 2018, if we look at the *percentage* of customers falling into each bin, the distributions of spend per customer, number of transactions, average spend per transaction, and profit per customer are, for all intents and purposes, the same.

Digging a bit deeper, there are some very minor changes. The average total spend per customer in 2019 ($183.16) was 0.7% lower than that for 2018 ($184.16). The average number of transactions per customer dropped by 1.8%, from 1.95 to 1.91. The mean average spend per customer increased from $97.58 to $98.21, a 0.6% increase. The average profit per customer increased a mere five cents, from $87.84 to $87.89. So does this imply that Madrigal's observed growth from 2018 to 2019 is solely attributed to the change in the number of customers (from 2.6 million to 3.2 million)?

The first questions to ask when faced with such customer counts for adjacent periods are "How many people were customers in both years?" and "How many customers only purchased in one year?" The answers to these questions are given in figure 4.2. The area of each circle is proportional to the number of customers each year, and the area of the overlap of the two circles is proportional to the number of customers active in both years. We see that 1,638,000 customers made at least one purchase in 2018 but none in 2019, 982,000 customers made at least one purchase in both years, and 2,203,000 customers only purchased in 2019, resulting in 4,823,000 unique customers across the two years.

The first thing that jumps out is that only 20% (982/4,823) of the 4.8 million customers who made a purchase over this two-year period made at least one purchase in both years. Similarly, only 37% (982/2,620) of the 2018 customers made at least one purchase in 2019. It may be tempting to think those customers who purchased in 2018 and not in 2019 are "lost." But it is too premature to draw that conclusion. It could be the case that they were one-time buyers, never to

Figure 4.1. The Four Basic Distributions for 2018 and 2019

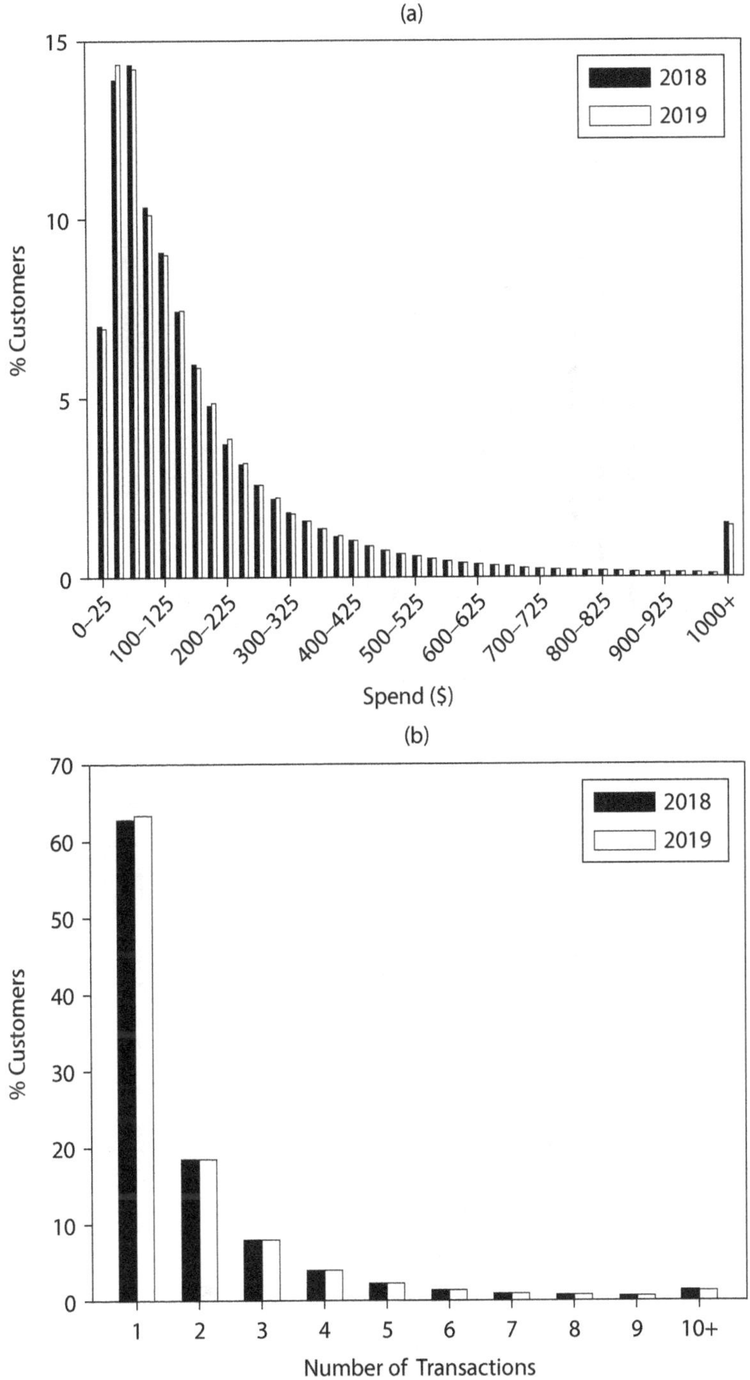

Figure 4.1. (continued)

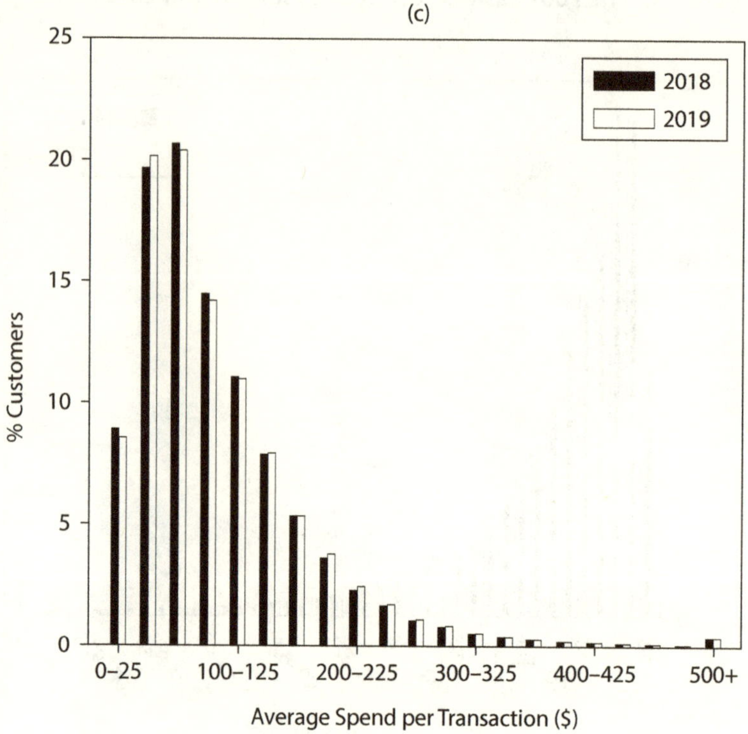

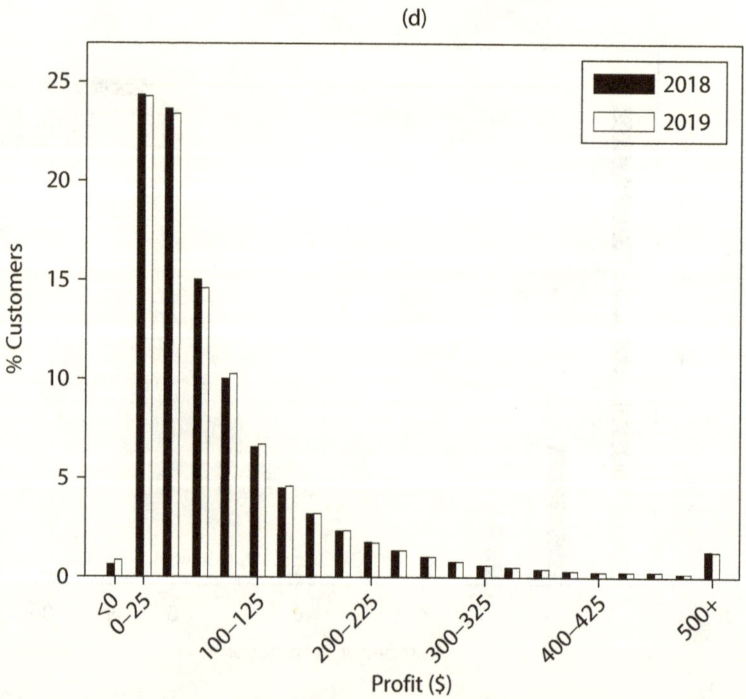

Figure 4.2. Overlap of the Customer Base in 2018 and 2019 (Customer Numbers in 000s)

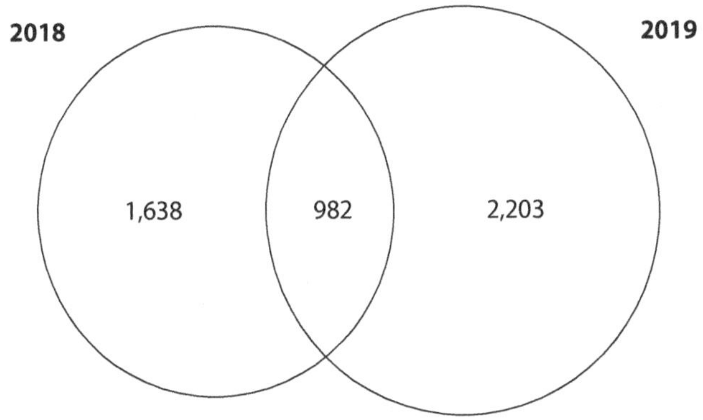

be seen again. Or it could be the case that they are simply light buyers; if, on average, you buy once a year, there will be some years in which you make no purchases. In reality, it will be a mix of both.

Similarly, it is tempting to think of those 2019-only customers as being "new." Some of them will be newly acquired customers, but others will be individuals acquired in previous years who simply did not make a purchase in 2018. (We will explore this further in chapter 5.)

Anyone who works in retail or who follows the performance of major retail stocks will be familiar with the idea of "same-store sales," also called "like-for-like sales." Recognizing that the opening of new stores can boost sales and give a misleading impression of the firm's overall performance, the idea of same-store sales is to compare the performance of stores that were open both this year and last year. This gives insight into the underlying performance of the business.

The same idea can be applied at the customer level. We can get a sense of "same-customer performance" by looking at the revenue and profit associated with those customers who made at least one purchase in both years.

As a starting point, figure 4.3 presents an additive decomposition of each year's profit into that attributable to those customers active in both years versus those active in just one of the two years.

Figure 4.3. Decomposition of Annual Profit ($million) by Customer Group

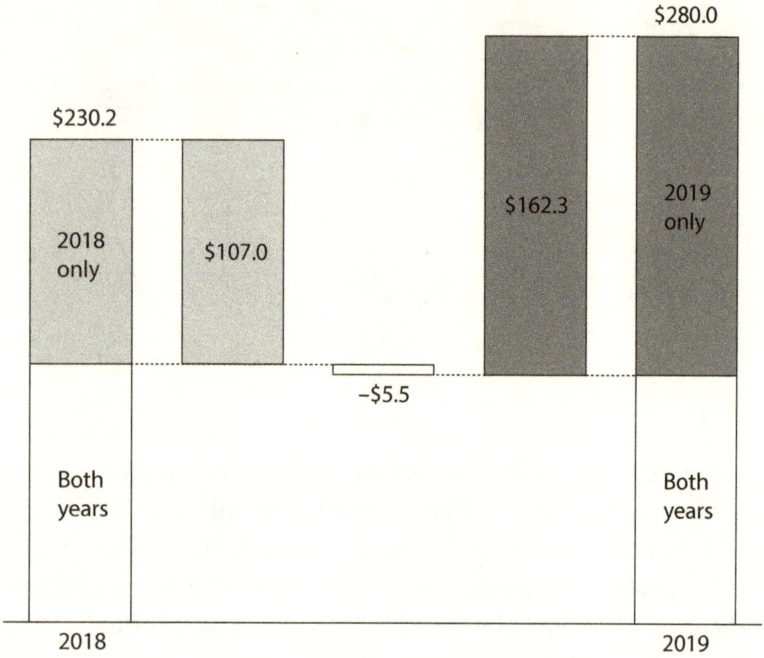

We see that the performance of the 2019-only group is over 50% higher than that of the 2018-only group ($162.3 versus $107.0 million). Is this simply due to the fact there were more people in the first group? And what lies behind the $5.5 million drop in profit for the group of customers that were active in both years?

To answer these questions, we make use of the multiplicative decomposition of profit introduced in the previous chapter: profit = # customers × AOF × AOV × average margin. The results of this decomposition for each of the three customer groups is reported in table 4.1.

Is the fact that the profit associated with the group of 2019-only customers is over 50% higher than that associated with the group of 2018-only customers simply down to the relative size of these two groups? No. We see that, on average, the 2019-only group also made

Table 4.1. Basic Temporal Decomposition of Performance

		2018	2019
2018 only	AOF	1.4	
(1.64 million customers)	AOV	$96	
	Avg margin	48%	
2019 only	AOF		1.5
(2.20 million customers)	AOV		$101
	Avg margin		48%
Both years	AOF	2.9	2.8
(0.98 million customers)	AOV	$93	$90
	Avg margin	47%	48%

slightly more transactions (AOF of 1.5 versus 1.4) and spent more per transaction (AOV of $101 versus $96). So, it is a combination of these three factors that lies behind the difference in the profit numbers.

What lies behind the $5.5 million decrease in profit associated with those customers active in both 2018 and 2019? While the AOF is down slightly (from 2.9 to 2.8), it would appear that most of this decline is due to the reduction in AOV (from $93 to $90).

Before diving deeper into the behavior of the group of customers active in both years, note that the AOF numbers for this group are substantially higher than those of both the 2018-only and 2019-only groups. Why would this be the case? As previously noted, a number of the 2018-only buyers are probably either one-time buyers, never to be seen again, or are simply light buyers. If you are a very light buyer, it is not very likely that you would make purchases in both years. Therefore, those that buy in both years are likely to have a higher buying rate, which is reflected in the AOF associated with this group of customers.

An Aside Regarding Averages

One takeaway from the Lens 1 analyses is that customers differ in behavior and value. In the previous chapter, we were disparaging about averages. How then can we justify our use of AOF and AOV?

These averages are the result of a multiplicative decomposition designed to help us understand the differences in, or the evolution of, a total (such as the profit associated with a group of customers in a given time period). They are not intended to summarize individual-level behavior. Their use is simply intended to give us a high-level yet insightful understanding of what lies behind the differences in the observed totals.

A deeper understanding of these differences can be obtained by undertaking analyses that do not start with the totals, but instead start with the individual customer-level data. We now turn our attention to two examples of such analyses.

Period-by-Period Changes in Customer Performance

To dig deeper into the variability in customer-level behavior and understand how it changes between 2018 and 2019, we undertake a modified decile analysis.

As we did in the decile analyses presented in the previous chapter, we begin by creating bins of customers that each represent 10% of the total profit in each year, from most profitable to least profitable. Rather than using separate profit decile cut-offs for each year, we use a common set of cut-offs for both years. The nine profit thresholds associated with the ten profit bins are \$559, \$358, \$259, \$196, \$151, \$117, \$89, \$65, and \$41. As a result of this, the associated profit bins do not account for exactly 10% of profit in each year.

We present in table 4.2 a cross-tabulation of decile membership in each year. (Decile 1 contains the most profitable customers.) Each cell in the body of the table shows the number of customers (in 000s) in each 2018 decile and 2019 decile bin. The core of the table describes

Table 4.2. Profit Decile Change (from 2018 to 2019)

		2019 Decile												
		1	2	3	4	5	6	7	8	9	10	2018 only	Total	% 2018 cust
2018 Decile	1	7	5	3	2	2	1	1	1	1	1	4	27	1%
	2	4	6	6	5	4	4	3	3	3	4	13	52	2%
	3	3	5	6	6	6	5	4	5	5	7	24	76	3%
	4	2	5	6	7	7	7	6	7	8	11	42	107	4%
	5	1	4	5	7	7	8	7	9	10	15	62	135	5%
	6	1	3	5	7	8	9	8	11	13	21	93	179	7%
	7	1	2	4	6	7	9	9	11	14	24	117	203	8%
	8	1	3	5	7	8	10	11	16	21	37	196	313	12%
	9	1	3	5	7	9	12	13	19	28	57	304	458	17%
	10	1	3	5	8	12	17	19	30	49	141	783	1069	41%
2019 only		10	25	44	70	98	140	169	271	400	977		2203	
Total		32	63	93	130	167	222	251	384	551	1294	1638	4824	
% 2019 cust		1%	2%	3%	4%	5%	7%	8%	12%	17%	41%			

decile switching of the 982,000 customers who made a purchase in both years.[4]

The diagonal of this table represents those customers who stayed in the same profit decile across the two years. Summing up the diagonal, we see that 236,000 of the 982,000 customers active in both years (24%) did not change profit decile.

How should we react to the fact that 76% of the customers changed their profit decile? The first thing to recognize is that some of these changes can be the result of very minor shifts in customer behavior. For example, those customers whose profitability lies between $358 and $559 are assigned to the second decile. If one customer's profit was $359 in 2018 and $357 in 2019, they would be one of the 6,000 customers who dropped from decile 2 to decile 3. Similarly, if their profit in 2018 was $558 and it increased to $560 the next year, they would be one of the 4,000 customers who rose from the second decile to the first decile.

Given the AOV and average margin numbers reported in table 4.1 for those customers active in both years, it is easy to see how making just one more or one fewer transaction in 2019 could result in a customer changing one or two deciles, especially in the case of the higher deciles (i.e., the less-profitable customers) where the decile boundaries are closer together.

We can therefore broaden the definition of the diagonal, looking at how many customers stayed within ± one decile between years. Counting the number of customers lying on this extended diagonal (the unshaded area in the table), we see that 49% (483/982) of those customers active in both years stay within plus-or-minus one decile between years.

Below this extended diagonal, the crosshatch-shaded area represents those customers who rose more than one decile, accounting for 24% (235/982) of those customers active in both years. The diagonal-shaded area above the extended diagonal represents those customers who dropped more than one decile, accounting for 27% (270/982) of those customers active in both years. This slight asymmetry is consistent with the fact that the value of those customers active in both years dropped by $5.5 million.

We tend to see this kind of slight period-to-period drop more often than we see a period-to-period increase, and we will explore this further when we lengthen the scope of the time frame in chapter 5 (when we discuss Lens 3).

The extreme changes in decile membership often warrant further investigation. For example, looking at the square of nine cells at the top right of the diagonal-shaded area, we see that 30,000 customers dropped from the top three deciles in 2018 (profit at least $259) to the bottom three deciles in 2019 (profit less than $89). Looking at the first three rows of the 2018-only column, we see that 41,000 of the customers in the top three deciles in 2018 did not make any purchases in 2019. It is worth investigating these two groups of customers. What lies behind this change in behavior?

Similarly, looking at the square of nine cells at the bottom left of the crosshatch-shaded area, 27,000 customers rose from the bottom three deciles in 2018 to the top three deciles in 2019. Can these changes be linked to any actions on the part of the firm?

Once again, we see the aforementioned asymmetry in action: There are more extreme jumps down than up (41,000 versus 27,000). Overall, these numbers are small (relative to the size of the overall customer base). While many of these cases might be one-time-only exceptions (e.g., a loyal customer who lived abroad for a year), they are still worth examining as one digs deeper.

That said, these changes should not distract our focus from the primary feature of table 4.2: its overall stability. Just under half of the customers active in both years (49% to be exact) can be found along the extended diagonal of the table. For the most part, the valuable customers remain valuable, and the not-so-valuable ones stay that way. This shows that the massive heterogeneity that we highlighted in the previous chapter tends to be reasonably enduring, all the more reason to look for it through the audit process, and to think carefully about how to manage it.

Drilling Down into Same-Customer Performance

As we seek to understand changes in customer-level profitability, a good starting point is to make use of a multiplicative decomposition of profit applied at the level of the individual customer. We can decompose a customer's annual profit into the product of number of transactions, average spend per transaction, and average margin.

For each customer, we ask the following four questions: Is their 2019 profit greater than or equal to their 2018 profit? Did they make the same or more purchases in 2019 compared to 2018? Is their 2019 average spend per transaction greater than or equal to their 2018 average spend per transaction? Is their average 2019 profit margin greater than or equal to their average 2018 margin? These four up/down (↑/↓) questions result in 16 possible groups of customers. We report in table 4.3 how many customers fall into each group and summarize their overall profit.

Looking at the first eight rows of the table, we see that 47% (464/982) of those customers active in both years saw their profit remain the same or increase in 2019. The total increase in their profit was $44.2 million. The remaining 53% (the next eight rows) saw their profit decline; the total decrease in their profit was $49.7 million, resulting in a net loss of $5.5 million.

Focusing on the 47% of the customers who maintained or increased their profitability to Madrigal, 63% (290/464) are associated with the first two rows of the table. These customers maintained or increased their number of transactions and average spend with the firm. With an average profit increase of $109, they account for 72% ((20.4 + 11.4)/44.2) of the $44.2 million increase in profit.

On the other hand, looking at those customers whose profitability decreased, the biggest single group of them actually increased their number of transactions, but their average spend per transaction and average margin both decreased enough to drag their profitability down overall. While accounting for a quarter of those customers who became less profitable, they only account for 14% (–7.1/–49.7) of the loss associated with these customers. Those customers associated

Table 4.3. Up-Down Analysis

Profit	# Trans	Avg spend/ trans	Avg margin	# Cust (000)	Profit ($MM) 2018	2019	Change
↑	↑	↑	↑	175	9.6	30.0	20.4
↑	↑	↑	↓	115	7.5	18.8	11.4
↑	↑	↓	↑	76	7.3	13.2	5.9
↑	↑	↓	↓	50	5.8	9.8	4.1
↑	↓	↑	↑	36	3.9	5.8	1.9
↑	↓	↑	↓	11	1.4	1.8	0.5
↑	↓	↓	↑	1	0.1	0.1	0.0
↑	↓	↓	↓	0	−0.0	−0.0	0.0
↓	↑	↑	↑	0	−0.0	−0.0	−0.0
↓	↑	↑	↓	15	0.9	0.7	−0.2
↓	↑	↓	↑	80	8.9	5.6	−3.3
↓	↑	↓	↓	129	15.3	8.2	−7.1
↓	↓	↑	↑	53	10.0	6.1	−4.0
↓	↓	↑	↓	51	9.3	5.0	−4.3
↓	↓	↓	↑	92	20.1	6.7	−13.4
↓	↓	↓	↓	98	23.1	5.7	−17.4
				982	123.2	117.7	−5.5
			2018 only	1,638	107.0	0.0	−107.0
			2019 only	2,203	0.0	162.3	162.3
			Total	4,823	230.2	280.0	49.8

with the bottom two rows (i.e., profit, number of transactions, and average spend per transaction are all down) account for 37% of those customers whose profit decreased and 62% ((−13.4 +−17.4)/−49.6) of the loss, with an average profit decrease of $162.

The two middle rows of this table may not make sense at first glance. How can a customer's profit increase between years when the number of transactions they made, their average spend per transaction, and their average margin decreased? In all cases, the firm made a loss on these customers in 2018. The reduction in the first two quantities meant that Madrigal made less of a loss on these customers, even though their average margin was lower (less of a loss means an increase in profitability). Similarly, how can a customer's profit decrease between years when the number of transactions they made, their average spend per transaction, and their average margin stayed the same or increased? These were also loss-making customers. While their negative average margin became less negative, an increase in the number of transactions and/or average spend per transaction meant that the loss associated with them increased.

As the idea of same-customer performance becomes an established performance measure, analyses such those presented in tables 4.2 and 4.3 should become routine.

Conclusion

As we saw at the outset of this chapter, a period-by-period analysis is far more than just repeating a Lens 1 analysis across multiple periods; that view (figure 4.1) is almost completely devoid of any meaningful insight (other than establishing the robustness of the basic Lens 1 patterns). Instead, the focus is on the differences from one period to the next, and from this perspective, the insights are abundant—especially when they build upon the analyses first set forth in the previous chapter.

Our principal observations about these changes can be summarized as follows:

- There is little stability in the set of active customers from one period to the next. Roughly 80% of customers who were active in the two-year span examined here were active in only one of the two years. This might come as a surprise but is actually quite normal.
- Those one-period-only customers tend to be less valuable than the 20% who remain active in both periods. In particular, their average order frequency is markedly lower, although their average order value is similar (actually slightly higher) for this dataset.
- For the two-period buyers, there is a slight drift downward in their profitability from one period to another. It is not dramatic overall, and there are abundant exceptions at the customer level, but this dynamic cannot be dismissed as a random blip.
- An up-down decomposition analysis reveals different insights for those customers who improved from 2018 to 2019 versus those who got worse. The majority of the former group showed clear improvements in both the number of transactions and average spend per transaction, but the results are mixed for the latter group. This particular outcome is likely idiosyncratic to this dataset, but it highlights the importance of performing such an analysis to understand the nature of the period-to-period changes.

Beyond these descriptive findings, there are also important strategic consequences arising from a Lens 2 perspective. For instance, suppose a company launched a tiered loyalty program that endows special privileges on its platinum customers. But in the next period, many of those customers do not make purchases, and even among those who do, they might do so less frequently or with lower average spend per transaction. Does this mean that the program is a failure? The results shown here demonstrate that such changes are often quite natural and should be expected. It is important for any such program to use future expectations instead of past history to gauge and guide program evaluation. Ditto for external events such as a health crisis or a macroeconomic shock (e.g., a recession). The Lens 2 analyses can help sort out the true incremental impact of such events from the natural baseline changes that we might expect to see under stable conditions.

Finally, we raise a parting question as a follow-up to the period-to-period comparisons we have covered here: What happens after Period 2? How do we analyze such data, and what should we expect to see over a longer horizon? Indeed, these are vitally important issues, and we will begin to address them in the next chapter. But just as Lens 1 gave us a foundation on which we could build Lens 2, the subsequent lenses will be a natural extension to the perspectives provided here. All of these lenses fit together in order to properly visualize and understand the customer base.

Executive Questions

- What kinds of "like-for-like" analyses do you currently conduct on a regular basis (e.g., same-store sales)? Are any of them performed at the customer level?
- Beyond the regular analyses, have you ever run a Lens 2–type project at the customer level to evaluate the impact of a particular event? Does your firm have the capability to do so?
- When you see customers seemingly "disappearing" from one period to the next, are you overreacting? What explanations do you offer, and what kinds of tactics do you engage in as a result (e.g., "customer win-back" campaigns)?
- Answer the same question(s) for the slight degradation in overall customer value for those customers who remain active through consecutive time periods: Are you willing to live with it, or do you take actions to try to stem the flow?
- Have you ever gone a step further to decompose these changes into their underlying components (i.e., number of transactions, average spend per transaction, average margin)? How are these components differentially affecting customer profitability?

Chapter 5

How Does Customer Behavior Evolve?

One takeaway from our Lens 2 analysis was that a portion of a firm's sales in a given year will come from customers who did not make a purchase in the previous year. Another takeaway was that a portion of the firm's customers in one year do not buy the next year. We were not willing to call the first group of customers "new" and the second group of customers "lost." We believe such labels represent extreme assumptions about the nature of each customer lurking in the firm's customer database.

If, as is increasingly the case, our transaction database tracks the buying behavior of each customer from their first purchase onward, we can identify which customers are truly new. This opens up an additional set of analyses that give us insight into the evolution of customer behavior and therefore the health of our customer base.

Central to these analyses is the notion of a "cohort," defined as the group of customers acquired in a particular period, be it a week, month, quarter, or year. When focusing on this group of customers, we can ask questions such as:

- How many ever come back and buy from us again?
- Of those who do come back, how does their buying behavior develop over time?
- Do they tend to buy more or less from us as they "age" as customers?

These questions, and more, are answered by a set of Lens 3 analyses, which summarize how the behavior of a single group of customers acquired in the same time period (i.e., one cohort) evolves over time, starting from their first-ever purchase from the firm.

Initial Analysis

In this chapter, we will focus on the group of 294,450 individuals who made their first-ever purchase from Madrigal in the first quarter of 2016. We will call this the Q1/2016 cohort. We have data on their purchasing through to the end of 2019 and will use it to illustrate a set of analyses that give us insight into the evolution of customer behavior.

Figure 5.1a is a plot of the weekly revenue associated with this cohort of customers over this four-year period. We see that weekly revenue rises quickly, fluctuates, and then drops precipitously to an underlying level that is less than 20% of its peak.

What is going on here? The answer lies in the point at which revenues plummet—the end of the first quarter of 2016. Up to that time, Madrigal was acquiring customers within the cohort, so its revenue was continually building. But after the cohort acquisition period ends, we are looking only at the ongoing repeat buying of those customers that comprise the cohort.

This becomes very clear in figure 5.1b, which separates total weekly revenue into that associated with the first purchases by the new customers (shaded) and that associated with their subsequent (or repeat) purchases (unshaded). We see that most of the revenue in the first quarter is associated with first-ever purchases, with the revenue attributable to repeat purchases growing slowly within that period. From the beginning of Q2/2016 onward, all of the cohort revenue is associated with repeat purchasing.

While it may not be obvious at first glance, the revenue associated with this cohort of customers is declining, despite clear seasonal uplifts associated with the fourth quarter of each year. This slow decline is a fairly general pattern that we see for most cohorts of most

Figure 5.1. Q1/2016 Cohort Weekly Revenue

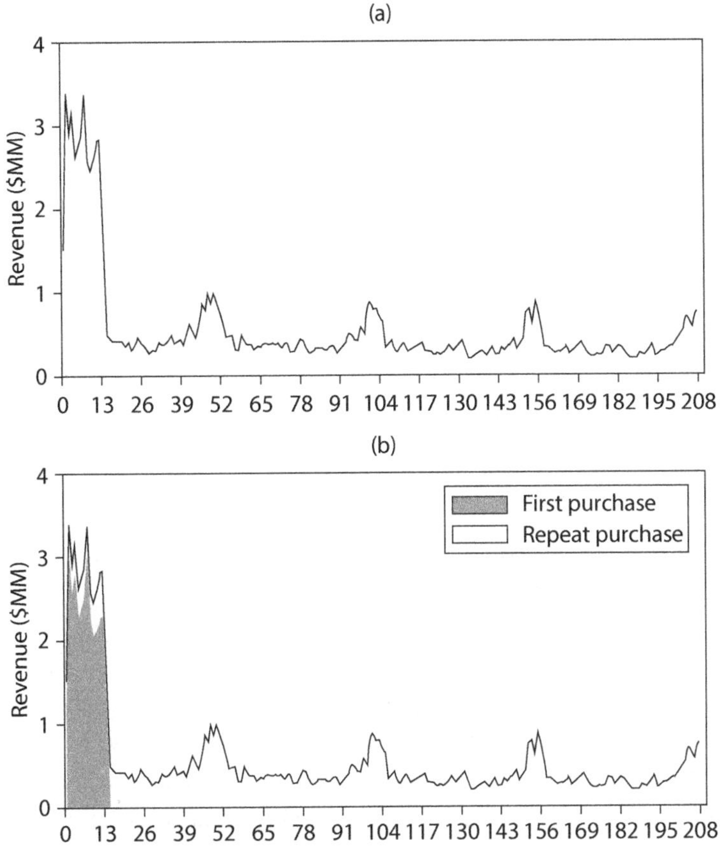

companies. This is consistent with the lower period-to-period purchasing described in Chapter 4 for the customers who were active in 2018 and 2019 (although that was not a cohort analysis).

Exploring the Underlying Patterns

As we seek to unpack what lies behind this general decline in repeat sales, the underlying patterns will be clearer if we move to a less granular unit of time. Figure 5.2 is a plot of the quarterly revenue associated with this cohort. The general decline in revenue is now clear.

Figure 5.2. Q1/2016 Cohort Quarterly Revenue

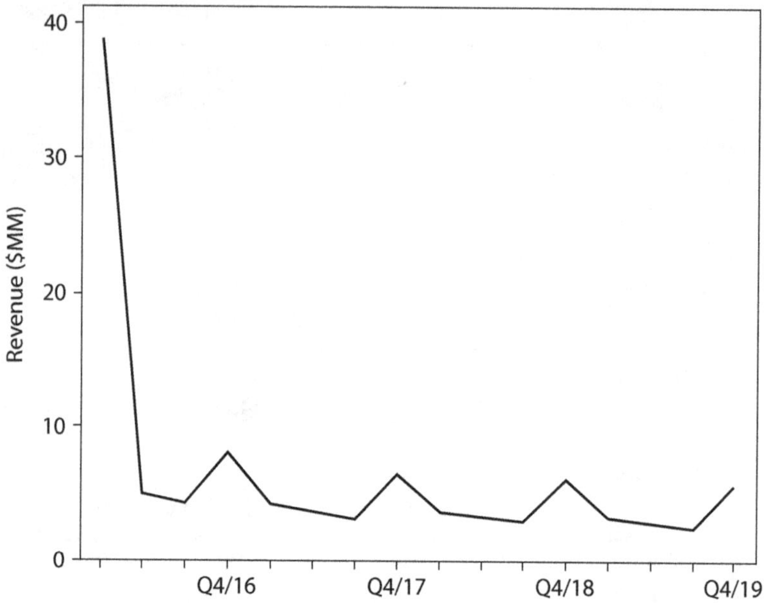

Our initial analysis of what lies behind these revenue patterns sees us making use of a multiplicative decomposition of revenue that is similar to the one we introduced in the previous chapters.

First, we recognize that not all the members of a cohort will buy in any given quarter. Therefore, the total revenue associated with a given cohort in a particular period of time (in this case, quarter) can be decomposed into the product of the number of cohort members who made at least one purchase that quarter, which we call active cohort members, and the average spend per active member:

$$\text{cohort revenue} = \begin{array}{c}\text{\#active cohort}\\\text{members}\end{array} \times \frac{\text{cohort revenue}}{\text{\#active cohort members}}$$

$$= \begin{array}{c}\text{\#active cohort}\\\text{members}\end{array} \times \begin{array}{c}\text{average spend per}\\\text{active cohort member}\end{array}$$

Second, rather than talking about the number of active cohort members in any given period of time, we will use the following identity, which recognizes that this quantity is simply the product of the number of people in the cohort (i.e., cohort size) and the proportion of cohort members making at least one purchase in that period of time:

$$\begin{aligned}\text{\#active cohort members} &= \text{cohort size} \times \frac{\text{\#active cohort members}}{\text{cohort size}} \\ &= \text{cohort size} \times \text{\% cohort active}\end{aligned}$$

Combining this with the decomposition of average spend into the product of average order frequency (AOF) and average order value (AOV) used in previous chapters gives us the overall decomposition of revenue associated with a cohort of customers in a given period of time presented in figure 5.3.

We apply the first part of this decomposition in figure 5.4, in which quarterly cohort revenue is decomposed into the product of cohort size, the percentage of cohort members active in each quarter, and the average spend per active cohort member for each quarter.

Figure 5.3. Multiplicative Decomposition of Period Revenue for a Cohort

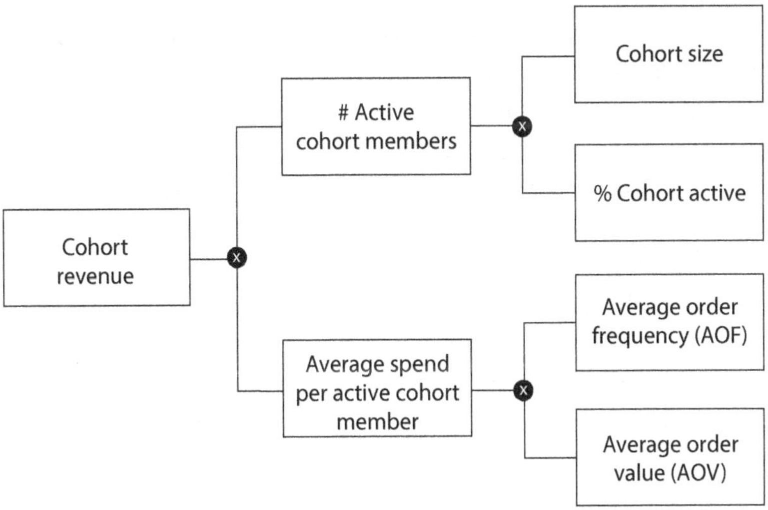

Figure 5.4. Multiplicative Decomposition of Q1/2016 Cohort Quarterly Revenue (Part 1)

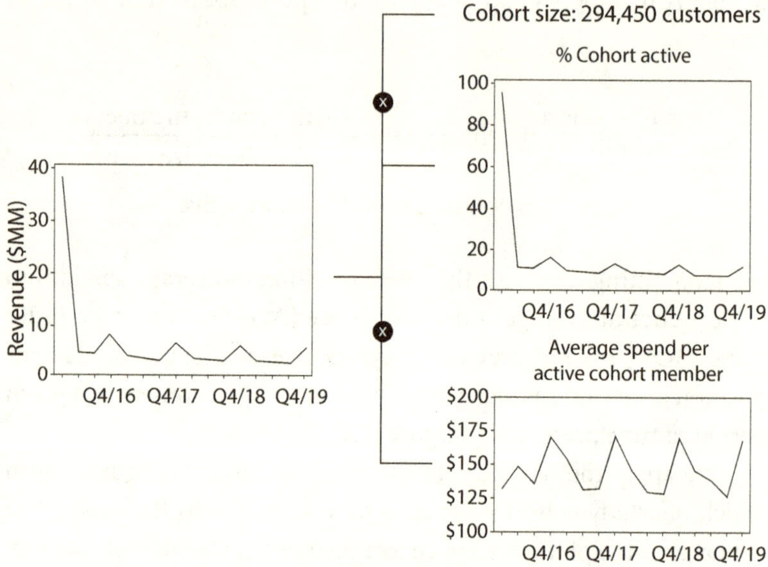

We immediately see that the seasonality in revenue (i.e., the Q4 revenue uplifts) is a function of two factors. First, there are more active cohort members in Q4. Second, those cohort members making at least one purchase in Q4 spend more on average than those cohort members making at least one purchase in other quarters. The general decline in revenue appears to be driven primarily by the slow underlying decline in the percentage of cohort members active in any period. Although it is not so strong, we also see a slight decline in average spend per active cohort member. While the Q4 average spend levels remain fairly constant, there is a slight decline in the Q2 and Q3 numbers over this period.

We apply the second part of this decomposition in figure 5.5, in which average spend per active cohort member is decomposed into the product of average order frequency (among those cohort members that made at least one purchase in that quarter) and the average order value. The Q4 spikes in average spend per active cohort member are a function of Q4 spikes in both AOF and AOV. Interestingly,

Figure 5.5. Multiplicative Decomposition of Q1/2016 Cohort Quarterly Revenue (Part 2)

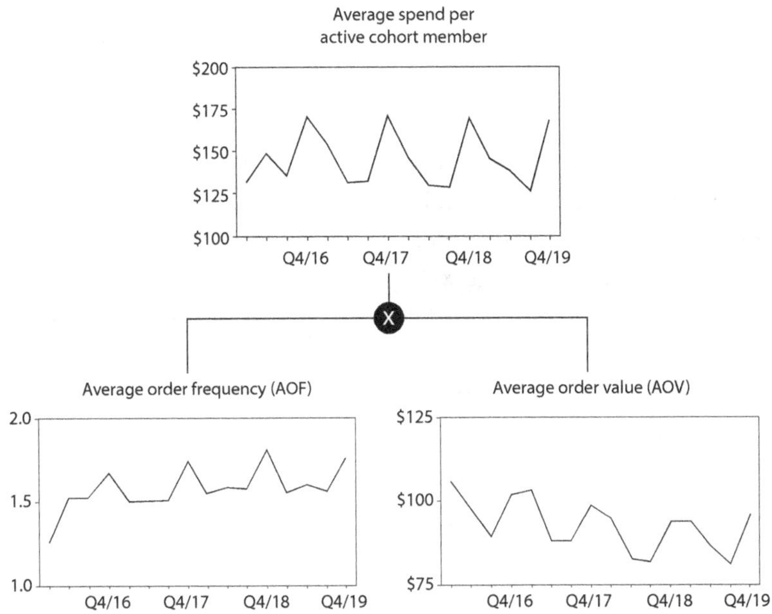

there is a slight increase in AOF over time, but this is dominated by a stronger decrease in AOV over time, which results in the previously noted slight decline in average spend per active cohort member.

Understanding the Evolution of Purchase Incidence

Looking at the plot of the percentage of the cohort that is active (figure 5.4), we see that, from Q2/2016 on, the percentage making a purchase in any given quarter ranges between 7% and 17%. What is behind this? Is it the case that, say, 80% of the cohort never make a second purchase and that the remaining 20% jump in and out of the market over the remaining quarters? Or is it the case that all the cohort members are "alive" and just buy very infrequently?

To answer this important question, we undertake the following analysis. For each member of the cohort, we ask whether they made a second purchase in 2016, at least one purchase in 2017, at least one purchase in 2018, and at least one purchase in 2019. There are 16 possible yes-or-no patterns, which, along with the percentage of the Q1/2016 cohort associated with each pattern, are reported in figure 5.6.

Three things jump out. First, looking at the N-N-N-N sequence, we see that 45% of customers acquired in Q1/2016 have not made a second purchase with Madrigal by the end of 2019. The presence of so many "one-and-done" customers frequently comes as a surprise to executives who have not looked carefully at customer cohort data, but it is actually a very common phenomenon.

Second, looking at the Y-N-N-N sequence, we see that 15% of those customers acquired in Q1/2016 made at least one other purchase in 2016 but none in the subsequent years. Taken together, this implies that 60% of customers acquired in Q1/2016 did not make another purchase in 2017–2019. In other words, all purchases in those three years were made by just 40% of the cohort.

Figure 5.6. Patterns of Annual Buying for the Q1/2016 Cohort

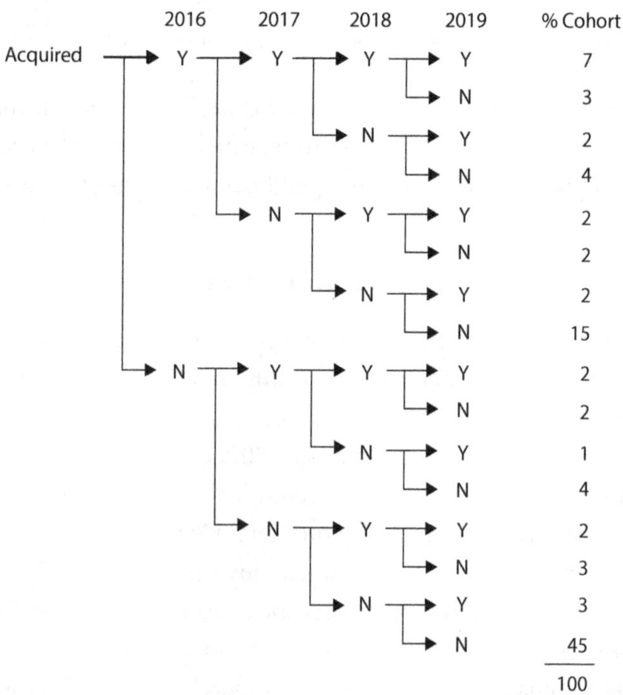

The third highlight is the Y-Y-Y-Y sequence: Just 7% of the cohort made at least one additional purchase sometime in 2016 and at least one purchase in each of the subsequent years.

Looking closely at figure 5.6, we note that 26% (100–7–3–4–15–45) of the cohort has an annual purchasing sequence in which the failure to make a (repeat) purchase in one year is followed by their making at least one purchase in a subsequent year. Lack of purchasing in one year does not mean the customer is "lost." This means we have to be very careful using terms such as "retained" or "retention" in settings such as this (more on this in chapter 9).

One metric we can consider is the (annual) repeat-buying rate, which tells us the percentage of the cohort active in one period (in this case, year) that make at least one purchase in the subsequent year. Counting from the top of figure 5.6, patterns 1–4 and 9–12 are associated with individuals who made at least one purchase in 2017. This corresponds to 25% of the cohort, which means we have a 2016–17 repeat buying rate of 25%. Of that 25% who had made at least one purchase in 2017, how many made at least one purchase in 2018? The percentage of the cohort associated with patterns 1–2 and 9–10 is 14%, so we have a 2017–18 repeat-buying rate of 56% (14/25). Similarly, 23% of the cohort made at least one purchase in 2018. Noting that 13% of the cohort are associated with patterns 1, 5, 9, and 13, we have a 2018–19 repeat-buying rate of 57% (13/23).

To reinforce the point against prematurely declaring a "lost" customer, we note 23% of the cohort made at least one purchase in 2018, and 14% of the cohort made at least one purchase in both 2017 and 2018. In other words, 39% (1–14/23) of the cohort members active in 2018 were inactive in 2017. This may seem surprisingly high and certainly motivates a more nuanced approach to defining a "lapsed" customer.

Returning to the observation that 55% of the cohort (those without the N-N-N-N pattern) did end up making a second purchase with the firm, how long did it take them to do so? In figure 5.7a, we plot the percentage of the cohort making their second-ever purchase in Q1/2016, Q2/2016, and so forth. We see that 17% made their second purchase in the same quarter in which they made their first purchase with the firm. A further 8% made their second purchase with the firm in Q2/2016, and so on. We see this declines rapidly, with ever-decreasing upticks in the fourth quarter of each year.

Figure 5.7b is a cumulative plot of these numbers, reporting the percentage of the cohort that have ever made a second-ever purchase by the end of each quarter. We see, for example, that 38% of the cohort had made a second purchase by the end of 2016. We may expect a few members of the cohort to make a second purchase beyond the end of 2019, but the likelihood is low. If we take 55% as a limit, we see that more than half of the cohort members who would eventually make a second purchase in this four-year period did so by the end of Q3/2016. The Q4 upticks are largely smoothed out in this cumulative curve, but there is still evidence that a group of customers end up making their second purchase sometime during a holiday season.

Should we be concerned by the fact that 45% of the Q1/2106 cohort never made a second purchase by the end of 2019? Obviously, the answer is "It depends," but on what does it depend?

A lot depends on the type of product or service you are selling. If you organize trekking holidays in the Himalayas or are a boutique hotel on a South Pacific island, it is understandable that you will be a once-in-a-lifetime purchase for the overwhelming majority of your customers. If you are a coffee shop in a small town with limited tourist traffic, you should be concerned. You need to reflect on the nature of your products or services and reflect on the nature of the differences in customer needs for your offerings.

Looking back at the AOF plot in figure 5.5, we note that the AOF was 1.24 in Q1/2016, noticeably lower than the AOF in any subsequent quarter.[5] As noted above, 17% of the cohort made at least a second purchase in Q1/2016. If each of those individuals had made just one extra purchase in that quarter, the Q1/2016 AOF would have been 1.17. The fact that it is larger suggests that some customers made three or more purchases in that first quarter. This raises the question of how long it takes for customers to make their third purchase (if ever),

Figure 5.7. Percentage of the Q1/2016 Cohort Making Their Second-Ever Purchase—(a) Quarter by Quarter and (b) Cumulative

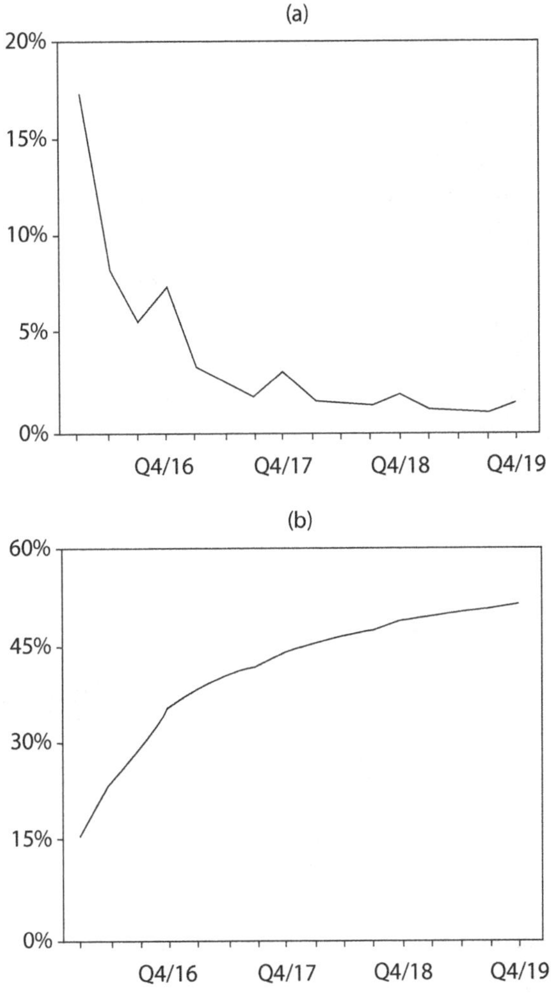

their fourth purchase, and so on, and how these "time to next purchase" patterns change the more purchases a customer makes.

In figure 5.7, we reported the proportion of the cohort members that had made a second repeat purchase. Someone who made their first purchase on the first day of Q1 and their second purchase on the last day of Q2 is viewed the same as someone who made their first purchase on the last day of Q1 and their second purchase on the first day of Q2.

To separate these two people, we can compute the time between each customer's first and (if observed) second purchase. The "1-to-2" line in figure 5.8 reports the percentage of the cohort that have made a second purchase 4, 8, . . . , 52 weeks after their first purchase. We see (as noted earlier) that 38% of the cohort made a second purchase within a year of their first purchase. Of those customers who made a second purchase within a year, more than half of them (21% of the cohort) had done so within 16 weeks of their first purchase.

We can also compute the time between a customer's second purchase (assuming they made one) and their third purchase (if observed by the end of Q4/2019).[6] Similarly, we can compute the time between a customer's third purchase (assuming they made one) and their

Figure 5.8. Cumulative Distribution of Time from One Purchase to the Next

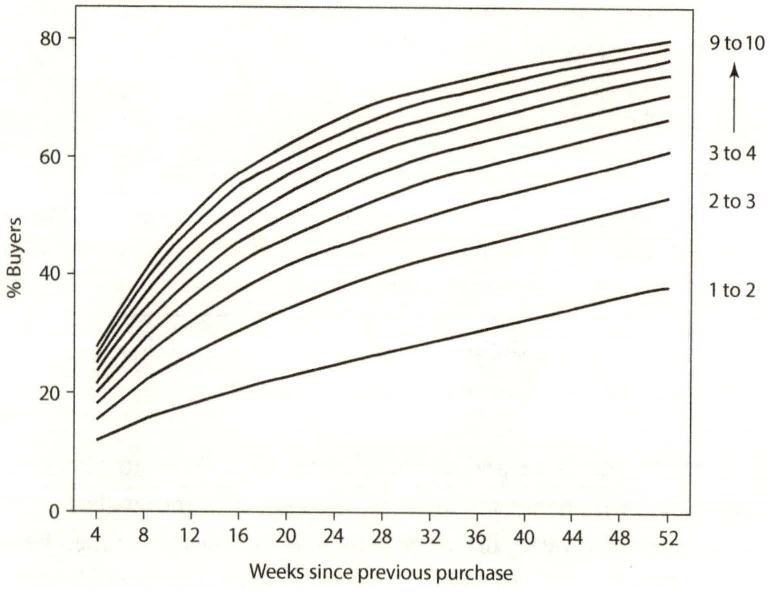

fourth purchase. And so on. Figure 5.8 reports the percentage of those that made their next purchase 4, 8, . . . , 52 weeks after their last one.[7]

Looking at this plot, we see that the curves have the same basic shape. However, they increase more quickly as the number of purchases made increases. The percentage making their next purchase within 52 weeks after their last purchase increases (albeit at a decreasing rate) the more purchases since acquisition we observe. So someone who has made seven purchases is more likely to make an eighth purchase within the next 52 weeks than someone who has made only two purchases.

There are two key points to keep in mind when interpreting this plot. First, customer heterogeneity plays an important role in understanding this pattern. The "base" for computing the "1-to-2" curve is all the cohort members. The "base" for the "2-to-3" curve is all those cohort members who had made a second purchase by the end of Q4/2018, so that we have a full year in which to observe whether they made a third purchase. Similarly, the "base" for the "9-to-10" curve is all those cohort members who had made a ninth purchase by the end of Q4/2018, so that we have a full year in which to observe whether they made a tenth purchase. Clearly, the group of people who have made nine purchases by the end of Q4/2018 are different from those who have made just two purchases in that time interval. The former group are by definition heavier buyers than the latter group, so the observation that their curve rises more quickly to a higher week-52 level should not be surprising.

The second point falls under the broad umbrella of not confusing association and causation. "Bribing" a customer to make a second purchase by offering them a very generous promotion probably does not change their underlying buying propensity: It likely will not lead them to buy more frequently and potentially increase their value to the firm. All it does is encourage them to wait around for the next generous promotion, which hurts profitability.

Many firms try to "cure" the one-and-done problem by incentivizing their customers to make repeat purchases. But the regularity of the patterns shown in figure 5.8—which is what we see for repeat purchasing for almost every company—shows that it is hard to change the "natural evolution" of repeat buying. Underlying differences across customers often proves to be a stronger and more enduring effect than marketing actions.

Exploring Differences in Customer Value

By now, we should have drilled into your mind the notion that customers are different. If that is true for a given period, then it is surely true—and maybe even more dramatic—when we look over a longer horizon. Thus, as we go from a single vertical slice of the customer × time face of the fundamental data cube (Lens 1) to a horizontal slice (Lens 3), it is natural to ask how the members of the cohort differ in their longer-term value to the firm. We will focus on their (undiscounted) profitability over the four-year period (2016–19), which we call value to date (VTD).

The VTD of individual cohort members ranged from a loss of $1,106 to a profit of $25,582. (The total VTD for this cohort is $50.5 million.) For cohort members whose profit over this four-year period was between $0 and $1,000, we count how many fall into $25-wide bins. We also create a bin for those customers on which the firm made a loss and a bin for those whose VTD is above $1,000. Figure 5.9 plots the percentage of cohort members falling into each bin.

Once again, we see a right-skewed distribution: 50% of the 294,450 individuals who made their first-ever purchase with Madrigal in the first quarter of 2016 had a VTD below $78; 73% had a VTD below the cohort average of $171.

To gain a high-level understanding of these differences, we perform a VTD-based decile analysis. We sort the 294,450 members of the cohort on the basis of their VTD, from most profitable to least profitable. The first decile comprises the most profitable members of the cohort who account for 10% of the cohort's total VTD. The second decile comprises the next most profitable members of the cohort who account for 10% of the cohort's total VTD. And so on.

Figure 5.9. Distribution of Q1/2016 Cohort VTD

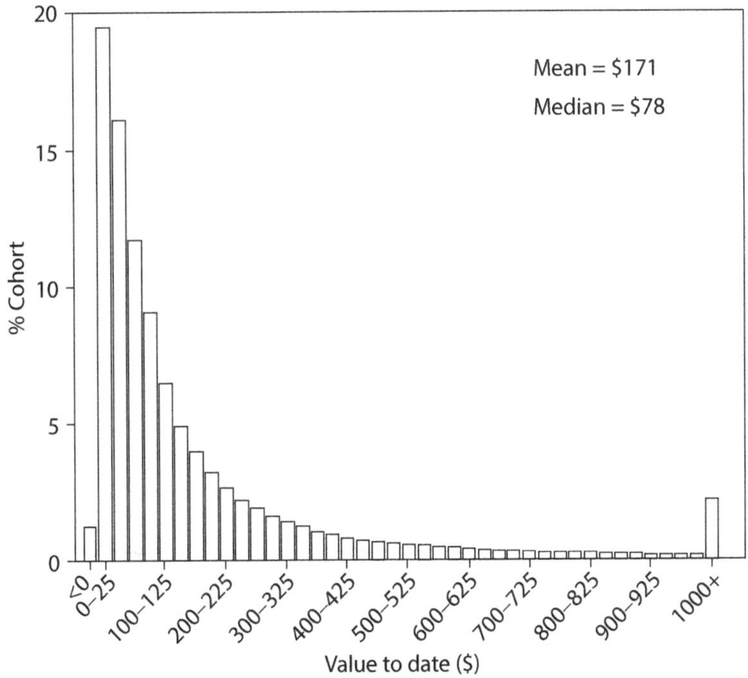

We report in table 5.1 the size of each decile along with a decomposition of the average VTD for each decile using the same multiplicative decomposition of decile value used in chapter 3.

Just under 11% of the members of the cohort (deciles 1–5) account for half the cohort's VTD. This is more concentrated than what was seen in the earlier profit-based deciles (table 3.4), with 15% of Madrigal's 2019 customers in the top-five deciles. While these numbers may not be dramatically different, they show that the nature/extent of heterogeneity seems to "stretch out" as the period of observation increases for a fixed cohort of customers.

While the more valuable deciles have higher AOF and AOV than the less valuable deciles, we see much greater variation in AOF across deciles—decile 1 is almost 26 times higher than decile 10—than we do in AOV, where decile 1 is just over two times higher than decile 10. How is this reflected in customer behavior over time?

Table 5.1. Summary of Cohort Behavior by VTD Decile

Decile	% VTD	% Cohort	% Trans	Avg VTD	AOF	AOV	Margin
1	10%	1%	7%	$2,441	36.3	$136	50%
2	10%	1%	8%	$1,247	20.5	$123	49%
3	10%	2%	8%	$842	14.6	$117	49%
4	10%	3%	9%	$609	11.1	$111	49%
5	10%	4%	9%	$451	8.6	$107	49%
6	10%	5%	9%	$334	6.6	$103	49%
7	10%	7%	10%	$243	5.0	$99	49%
8	10%	10%	10%	$168	3.7	$94	48%
9	10%	16%	11%	$105	2.5	$89	48%
10	10%	51%	20%	$34	1.4	$59	40%
				$171	3.7	$97	48%

We report in table 5.2 the percentage of the cohort associated with each decile that are active in each calendar year. Not surprisingly, the more valuable members of the cohort are more active each year, thereby reinforcing the idea that differences across the customers in a cohort are further accentuated as time passes.

Of course, it must be noted that, in absolute terms, more members of the 10th decile were active in 2019 than members of the first decile (5% of 51% is bigger than 90% of 1%). So, we have to be careful about "writing off" low-value customers too quickly.

Taking Stock: RFM Analysis

The analyses presented above describe how the behavior of a cohort of new customers evolves over time. Standing at the end of 2019, how can we take stock of this cohort of customers?

One approach that has its origins in the age of catalog retailing is the so-called RFM analysis.

Table 5.2. Annual % Active by VTD Decile

Decile	% Cohort	2016	2017	2018	2019
1	1%	100%	95%	94%	90%
2	1%	100%	91%	90%	84%
3	2%	100%	85%	84%	78%
4	3%	100%	79%	75%	70%
5	4%	100%	70%	66%	61%
6	5%	100%	60%	55%	50%
7	7%	100%	50%	44%	40%
8	10%	100%	37%	32%	29%
9	16%	100%	22%	19%	16%
10	51%	100%	7%	6%	5%

- R stands for **recency**. For each cohort member, we note when they made their last purchase. In this example, we note the quarter in which their last purchase occurred.
- F stands for **frequency**. For each cohort member, we note how many transactions they made with Madrigal over this four-year period.
- M stands for **monetary value.** This could be interpreted as spend or profit. In this case, we will focus on profit. For each cohort member, we note their average profit per transaction over this four-year period.

We first segment the members of the cohort on the basis of recency: Was their last purchase in Q1 (Q1/2016), Q2-Q8 (Q2/2016-Q4/2017), Q9-Q15 (Q1/2018-Q3/2019), or Q16 (Q4/2019)? We then segment the members of the cohort on the basis of frequency: Did they make just one purchase in the past four years, 2–4 purchases, 5–10 purchases, or 11 or more purchases? Finally, we segment the members of the cohort on the basis of their average profit per transaction: Was it less than $25, between $25 and $50, between $50 and $75, or greater than $75?[8]

With four recency categories, four frequency categories, and four monetary value categories, there should be 64 possible RFM segments. However, in this application, there are only 52 feasible combinations, as anyone with a frequency of 1 cannot have made a purchase any later than Q1/2016. In table 5.3, we report the number of cohort members associated with each of the feasible RFM combinations.

Table 5.3. RFM Summary for the Q1/2016 Cohort (Customer Numbers in 000s)

		Frequency			
Recency	Avg profit per trans	1	2–4	5–10	11+
Q1	<25	52.9	6.6	0.1	0.0
	25–50	33.5	5.4	0.1	0.0
	50–75	19.2	3.1	0.0	0.0
	75+	27.5	3.6	0.0	0.0
Q2-Q8	<25		11.6	1.5	0.1
	25–50		14.3	2.5	0.2
	50–75		8.5	1.6	0.1
	75+		8.6	1.3	0.1
Q9-Q15	<25		7.9	4.9	1.7
	25–50		10.0	8.9	3.0
	50–75		5.8	5.0	1.6
	75+		4.8	3.3	1.0
Q16	<25		2.0	2.5	3.2
	25–50		3.1	5.4	5.6
	50–75		1.8	3.0	2.8
	75+		1.5	2.0	1.3

In light of the analyses presented earlier in this chapter, it is not at all surprising to see that the bulk of the cohort resides in the upper-left portion of the table (i.e., low recency and/or low frequency). Remember that 45% of the cohort has not made a second purchase by the end of 2019, and therefore have a frequency of 1. But it might come as a surprise that the least-populated part of the table is right next to it (in the upper right). The changes across the columns for the upper part of the table are much greater than in the lower sections, but it makes sense: Very heavy buyers were almost certainly active in periods beyond Q1/2016.

The very few buyers in the upper right (e.g., the roughly 100 customers with frequency of 5–10 and average profit per transaction of $25–$50) used to be very good customers, but they appear to have dropped out since the initial quarter of acquisition. In some sense, they are an even more extreme version of one-and-done customers—perhaps even less likely to come back again, given how active they used to be.

Finally, note that most of the "action" for this table is associated with changes in recency and frequency, not monetary value. This reflects some of our earlier discussion (for Lens 1) that spend levels are largely independent of the flow of transactions. It also reinforces the relevance of the particular name for this rubric: RFM. The order of those letters is not a coincidence: recency and frequency are much more important/diagnostic than monetary value. That is not to say that the latter is unimportant. Not at all. It belongs in this trinity of key summary metrics, but in third place. Spend and profit levels might be more visible than (and trigger stronger managerial reactions than) recency metrics, but a careful customer-base audit objectively reflects their true importance.

Conclusion

From a purely methodological/analytical perspective, it may seem that Lens 3 is not very different from Lens 1; one could (incorrectly) say that all we have done with Lens 3 is stretched out the time window. But there is much more going on here.

First and foremost, there is a critically important distinction between the scope of Lens 1 and that of Lens 3: With Lens 1, we looked at all those customers active in 2019, regardless of when each customer was acquired. In some sense, we were mixing apples and oranges because we were not distinguishing between new customers and long-tenured ones. With Lens 3, in contrast, we are only focusing on a well-defined cohort of customers who were acquired at (approximately) the same time. Accounting for this difference is essential.

So it is useful to apply (and then go beyond) the kinds of static analyses we covered in Lens 1 to the long-run vantage point that Lens 3 offers. We see that the initial heterogeneity observed in Lens 1 is amplified as the one-and-done customers drop out and the more valuable ones stay active. But even the valuable ones have some interesting patterns of heterogeneity and time dynamics among them, as seen in our decompositions and exploration of the times between successive purchases.

The Lens 3 cohort analysis is positioned literally and figuratively at the center of a customer-base audit, so the distinctions between it and the other lenses should not be blurred. For our next step, we go back to the spirit of the Lens 1 to Lens 2 transition to motivate the importance of comparing subsequent cohorts; that is what Lens 4 will focus on, and Lens 5 will build upon.

Executive Questions

- What technologies or marketing programs do you rely on to "tag and track" your newly acquired customers to facilitate a cohort analysis?
- When you engage in different kinds of promotions and other kinds of customer-focused campaigns, do you evaluate them purely in a period-to-period manner (as in Lens 2), or do you look for ongoing effects that may persist over longer horizons for a given cohort?
- Do you provide any regular reports (to internal or external stakeholders) that reflect cohort-level behaviors?

- We have only focused on time-based cohorts. But do you examine other kinds of cohorts, grouping customers on other acquisition characteristics such as channel, product(s), or campaign associated with their first purchase in addition to their period of acquisition?
- Do you try to actively measure/manage the (apparent) one-and-done customers? How much (and for how long) do you invest in them to become ongoing repeat buyers, and at what point (if ever) do you give up on them?
- Does your organization conduct RFM-based segmentation? What do you do with these segments once you create/identify them? How does this kind of segmentation scheme compare (or interact) with other bases of segmentation that you may rely upon?

Chapter 6

Comparing and Contrasting Cohort Performance

One of the most immediate and important observations that arises in a customer-base audit is that all customers are not created equal. This has been a major theme throughout this book. But the same can be said for cohorts of customers: While it is vital to understand the overall quality of (and the dynamics that occur within) a given cohort, it is often the differences across cohorts that tell us more about the current and future health of the customer base (and thus the organization) as a whole.

Every growth-oriented firm is constantly seeking new customers, but the customer-centric firm will focus at least as much on the *quality* of the next batch of customers as they will on the *quantity* of them. With this in mind, we build on what we covered in the last chapter, using it as a foundation for making such comparisons. For the sake of clarity, we will focus on comparing two cohorts at a time, then expand further in the next chapter.

Let us consider two (quarterly) cohorts of customers acquired by Madrigal in 2016, in Q3 and Q4. The quarterly profit associated with these two cohorts is reported in figure 6.1.

It is difficult to make meaningful comparisons between the two cohorts simply by looking at the raw numbers, aside from the fact that the Q4 cohort as a whole is of greater value to Madrigal—and that observation could be somewhat misleading.

One thing that many firms starting to take a cohort-based view of their business will do is index the profit associated with each cohort

Figure 6.1. Quarterly Profit Associated with the Q3/2016 and Q4/2016 Cohorts

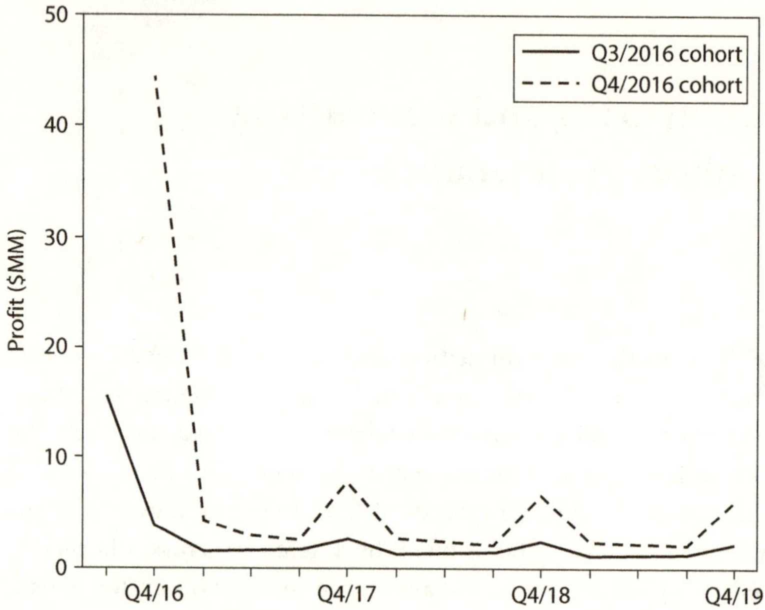

in each period relative to the profit associated with their acquisition period. We report the associated numbers for these two cohorts in figure 6.2.

What do we learn from such a plot? Aside from the fact that the Q3/2016 cohort "retains" a greater level of its initial acquisition quarter profit over time than the Q4/2016 cohort, not much. We cannot even say that the average Q3/2016 cohort member is worth more than the average Q4/2016 cohort member.

Any investigation of how the cohorts differ should start with the customer being the unit of analysis. In our discussion of Lens 3, we examined a multiplicative decomposition of cohort-level revenue over time that is possible given a knowledge of how many members of the cohort were active in each period. In figure 6.3, we extend this to give us a multiplicative decomposition of cohort-level profit.

Madrigal acquired about 284,000 new customers in the third quarter of 2016 and about 616,000 new customers in the fourth

Figure 6.2. Quarterly Profit Associated with the Q3/2016 and Q4/2016 Cohorts Indexed Against Acquisition-Quarter Profit

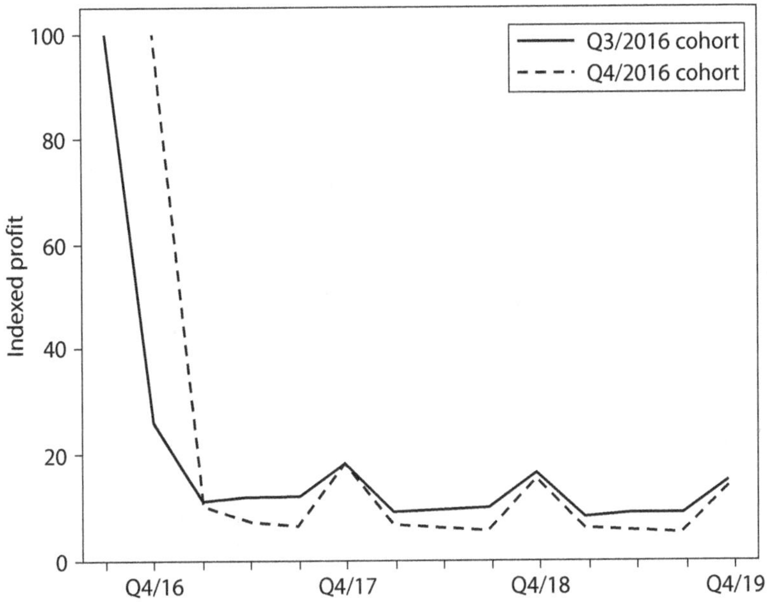

quarter. This alone could explain the difference in profit shown in figure 6.1, so it is important to get past the aggregate data to understand what is really going on.

Controlling for differences in cohort size, we first examine the evolution of % cohort active, AOF, AOV, and average margin. We plot these four quantities over time for each cohort in figures 6.4–6.7.

Let us first consider how the cohorts differ in terms of the percentage of cohort members that are active in any given quarter. We see in figure 6.4 that both cohorts quickly drop to similar percentages for this metric. There are, however, two minor differences. First, we see greater seasonality for the Q4 cohort. A slightly higher percentage of the cohort members are active in Q4 compared to the Q3/2016 cohort, while they are less active in the other three quarters of each year. Second, the percentage of cohort members that are active the quarter immediately after the quarter of acquisition is

Figure 6.3. Multiplicative Decomposition of Period Profit for a Cohort

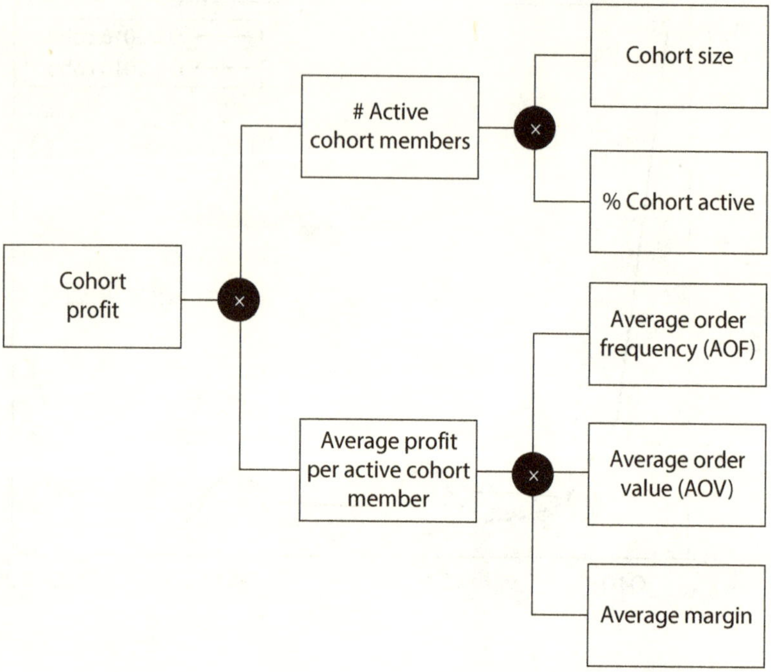

higher for the Q3/2016 cohort than for the Q4/2016 cohort. This reflects the general seasonality in the % cohort active metric. While there is a general decline over time, we see blips in Q4, reflecting holiday season purchasing at Madrigal.

Turning our attention to the evolution of AOF (figure 6.5), there is a noticeable difference between the two cohorts early in their "life" as customers of Madrigal. The lower-than-average AOF in the first quarter of each cohort (1.2 for Q3/2106 and 1.3 for Q4/2016) reflects the fact that a large chunk of new customers only ever make one purchase from Madrigal. The slightly higher first-period AOF for the Q4/2016 cohort suggests that the cohort members that make a repeat purchase do so at a slightly faster rate. This reflects the general seasonality in buying behavior, which is also reflected in the jump in

Figure 6.4. Percentage of the Q3/2016 and Q4/2016 Cohort Members Active Each Quarter

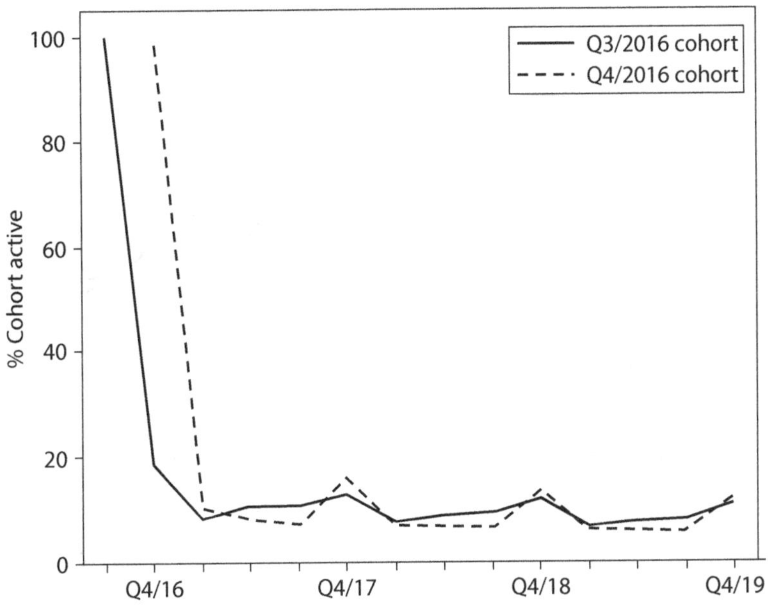

Figure 6.5. Evolution of AOF for the Q3/2016 and Q4/2016 Cohorts

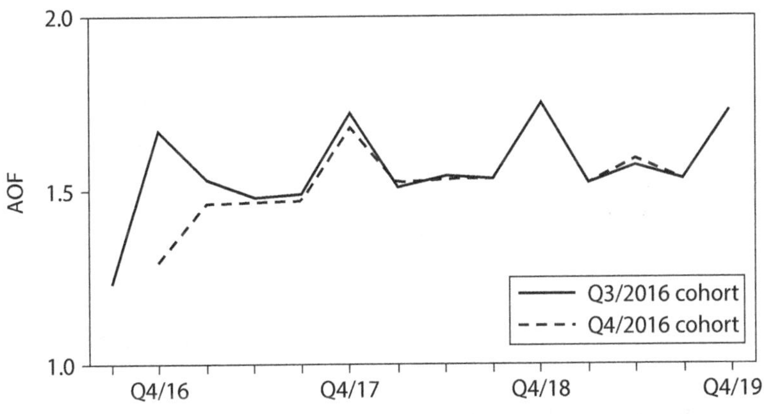

Figure 6.6. Evolution of AOV for the Q3/2016 and Q4/2016 Cohorts

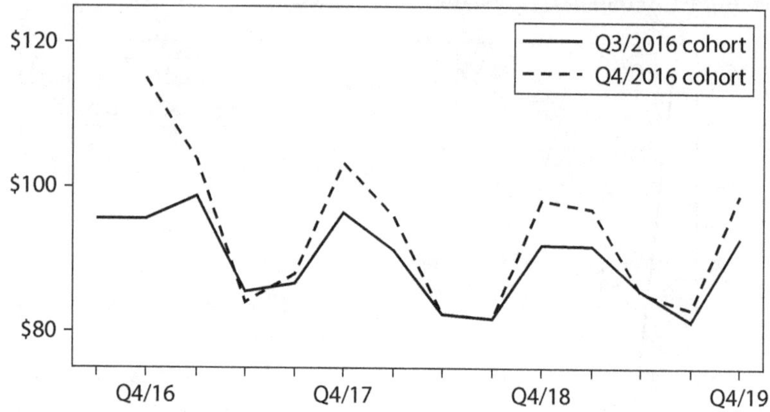

Figure 6.7. Evolution of Average Margin for the Q3/2016 and Q4/2016 Cohorts

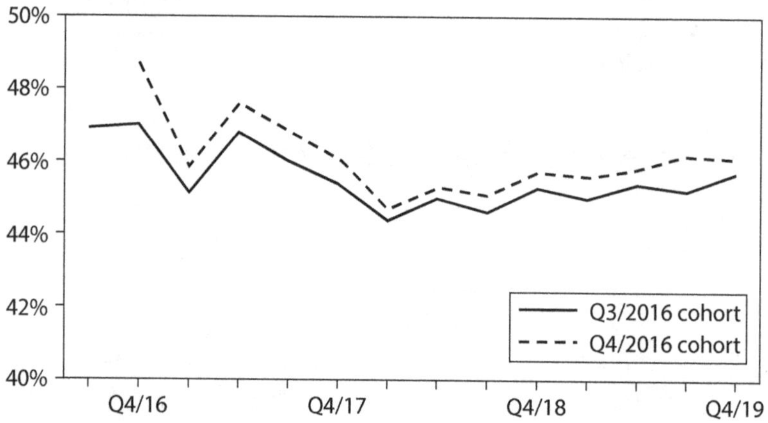

AOF from Q3/2016 to Q4/2016 for the Q3/2016 cohort. Despite these early differences, the two soon become very similar in terms of the AOF of their active customers.

How do the active members of each cohort differ in terms of their AOV? Looking at figure 6.6, we observe seasonality and a general decline in AOV over time. However, we do observe two key differences. Those customers acquired in Q4/2016 are spending noticeably more per transaction in their first quarter with Madrigal. While their AOV is slightly higher than that of the Q3/2016 cohort in subsequent first and fourth quarters, it is basically the same in the second and third quarters.

Finally, looking at average margin (figure 6.7), we see that the two cohorts are consistently different, with members of the Q4/2016 cohort having a higher average margin per transaction than the members of the Q3/2016 cohort. What lies behind this? Is it because these cohort members are buying a different mix of products that have different margins? Do they differ in terms of their propensity to buy products on promotion? We would need to dig deeper into the data to get a sense of why we see this difference. While such an investigation is definitely worthwhile, it may be getting into too much detail for a high-level customer-base audit.

Reflecting on the observed differences between these two cohorts, it seems reasonable to infer that many of the effects just described can be attributed to the fact that one cohort was acquired during the holiday period (Q4) while the other was not. With this in mind, we now repeat a similar exercise for two cohorts acquired during the same quarter but in different years.

As an illustration, let us consider the cohort of customers Madrigal acquired in Q4/2016 and compare it to the cohort acquired in Q4/2017. The quarterly profits associated with these two cohorts are plotted in figure 6.8.

As noted above, the Q4/2016 cohort comprises 616,000 customers. Once we control for the fact that the Q4/2017 cohort is slightly smaller (589,000 individuals), how do these two cohorts differ?

We apply the same multiplicative decomposition of profit as used above. However, we will make a slight change to how we present the associated numbers. Rather than the x-axis representing calendar time, which means the line associated with the Q4/2017 cohort is shifted four quarters to the right of that associated with the Q4/2016 cohort, we will focus on the "age" of each cohort. In other words, we left-align the lines associated with each cohort, so we can see whether the evolution of a cohort's behavior from its "birth" is the same as

Figure 6.8. Quarterly Profit Associated with the Q4/2016 and Q4/2017 Cohorts

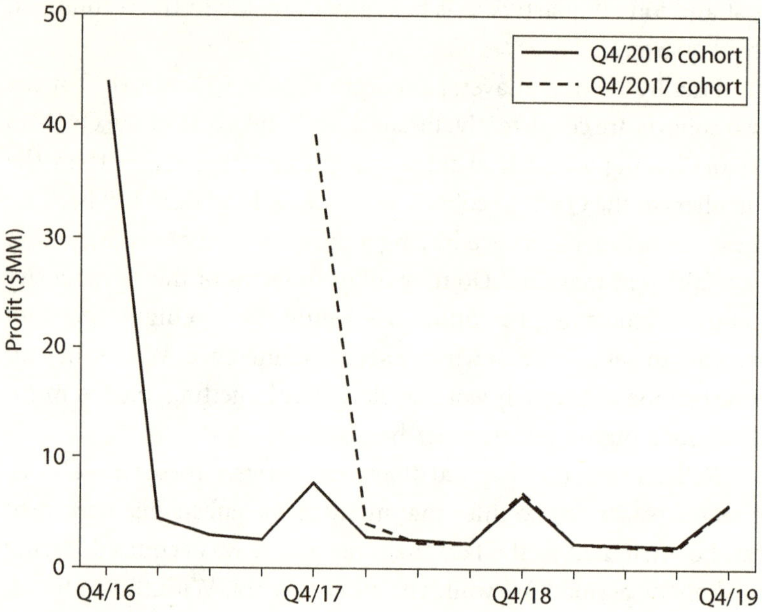

that of other cohorts. When there is strong seasonality in buying behavior, as is the case for Madrigal, the plots will be clearer if we left-align the numbers for cohorts born in the same period in each season (in this case, Q4).

In figure 6.9, we plot the evolution of the percentage of cohort members that are active each quarter for these two cohorts. The consistency in the cohort-level pattern may be surprising for many. We are looking at two groups of customers acquired 12 months apart, yet they "age" in almost exactly the same way as we consider the percentage of cohort members making at least one purchase in any subsequent quarter.

Looking at the evolution of average order frequency (figure 6.10) and average order value (figure 6.11) among the active members of each cohort over time, we see some differences, but they are not especially large or systematic (especially when compared to the previous cross-cohort comparison in figures 6.5 and 6.6).

Figure 6.9. Percentage of the Q4/2016 and Q4/2017 Cohort Members Active Each Quarter

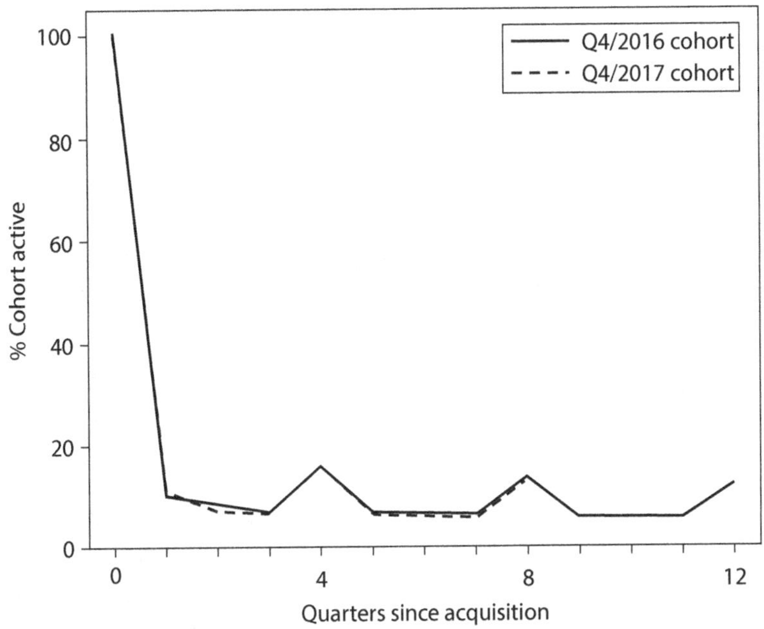

Figure 6.10. Evolution of AOF for the Q4/2016 and Q4/2017 Cohorts

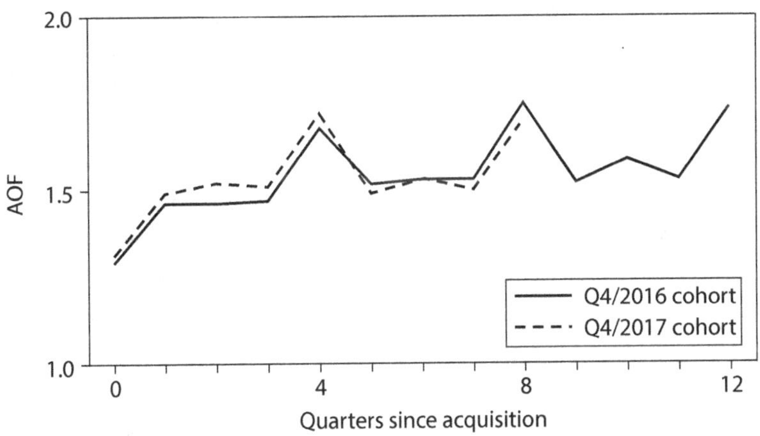

Figure 6.11. Evolution of AOV for the Q4/2016 and Q4/2017 Cohorts

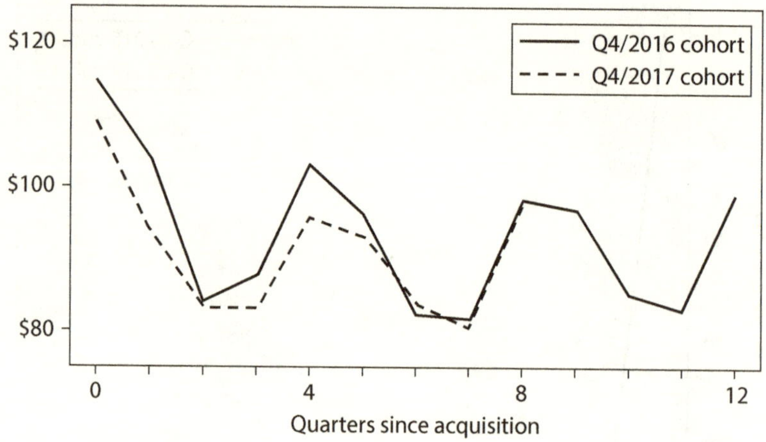

Finally, we look at differences in the evolution of average quarterly margin (figure 6.12). This is clearly the biggest difference we have seen for these two cohorts, so a natural question is whether there has been any change in Madrigal's pricing and promotion policies in the year between Q4/2016 and Q4/2017.

In figure 6.13, we plot the same numbers where the x-axis of the plot goes back to calendar time (i.e., quarters) instead of being left-aligned. Now the differences are far less pronounced. The overall drop in margin from Q4/2016, and then its gradual rise, seems to suggest changes in Madrigal's pricing and promotion policies over time as opposed to the changing nature of the cohorts.

Beyond a demonstration of the basic profit decomposition framework, we can also perform cohort comparisons for the other types of cohort-level analyses discussed in the previous chapter. For example, one way to understand the development of repeat buying is to look at how long after their first purchase a new customer makes their second purchase, if ever.

Returning to our comparison of the Q3/2016 and Q4/2016 cohorts, we plot in figure 6.14 the cumulative percentage of cohort members that have made their second purchase within a year of being

Figure 6.12. Evolution of Margin for the Q4/2016 and Q4/2017 Cohorts

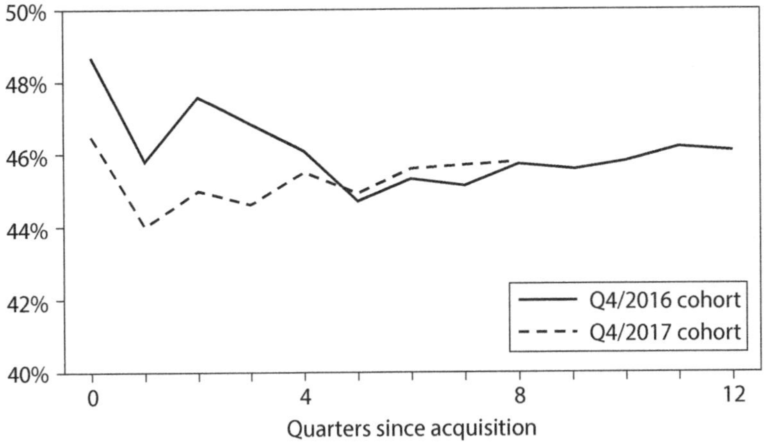

Figure 6.13. Evolution of Margin for the Q4/2016 and Q4/2017 Cohorts (Time Aligned)

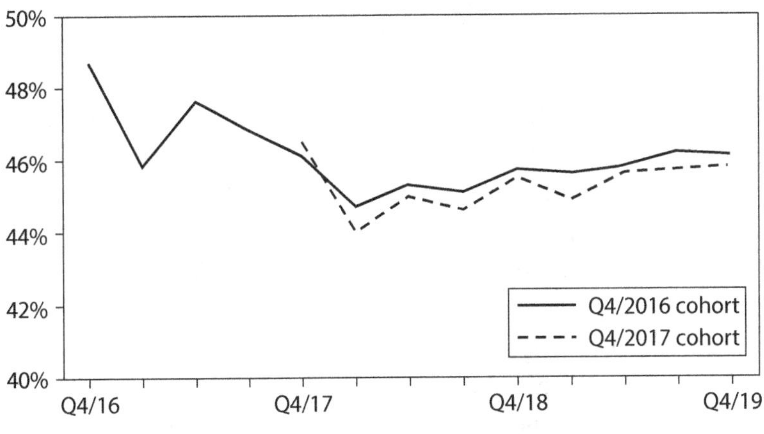

acquired. We see that 35% of the Q3/2016 cohort had made at least one repeat purchase within that year. This is slightly lower for the Q4/2016 cohort, with 33% of the cohort making a repeat purchase.

To better understand the evolution of repeat buying in these two cohorts, we can look at an incremental (period-by-period) version of

Figure 6.14. Comparing the Cumulative Distribution of Time to Second Purchase for the Q3/2016 and Q4/2016 Cohorts

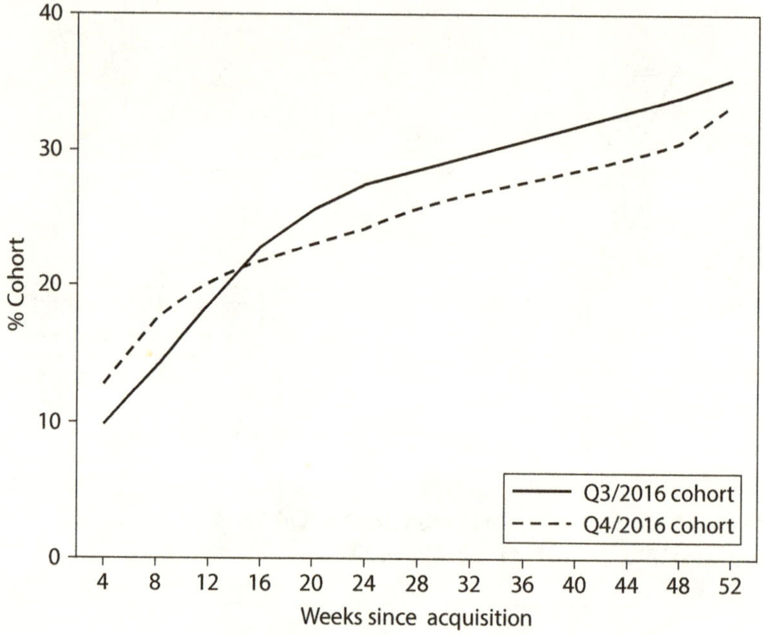

this plot. In figure 6.15, we plot the percentage of the cohort that made their second-ever purchase from Madrigal in the first four weeks following their first purchase, in the second four weeks following their first purchase, and so on.

We notice that a greater proportion of the Q4/2016 cohort made a repeat purchase within four weeks of their first purchase. This is perhaps not surprising given the seasonality we have observed earlier. For this same reason, the uptick we observe 49 to 52 weeks after the first purchase is also not surprising. We have a group of cohort members who are regular holiday season buyers, but they do not do much for the rest of the year.

While the number of people making a second purchase drops off quickly for the Q4/2016 cohort, we do not see such a rapid decline in the Q3/2016 cohort, with a group of customers making their second purchases from Madrigal 12 to 20 weeks later (i.e., during the

Figure 6.15. Comparing the Number of Weeks Taken to Make a Second Purchase for the Q3/2016 and Q4/2016 Cohorts

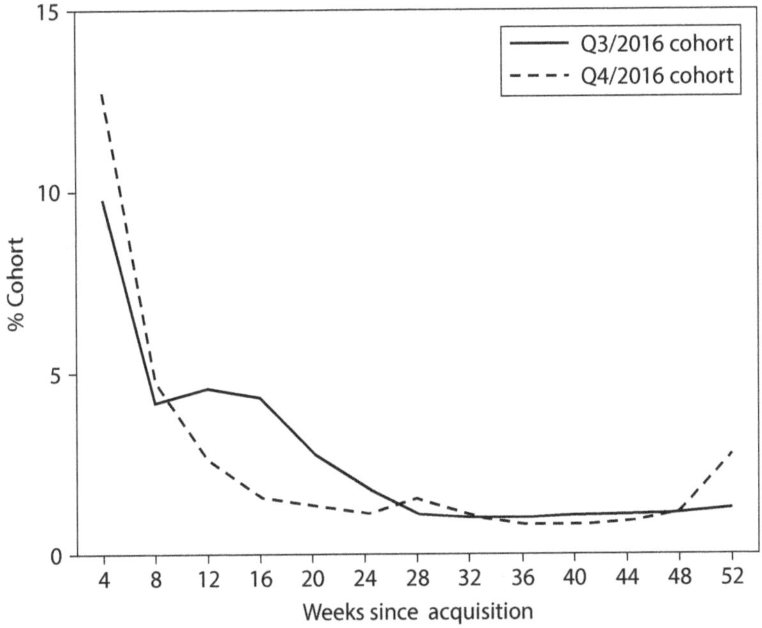

holiday period). This shows that the compositions of the two cohorts are fairly different, and in ways that are relevant and actionable for Madrigal.

Contrast this to the comparison of the Q4/2016 and Q4/2017 cohorts (figures 6.16 and 6.17). Aside from a slight difference in the proportion of the cohort members making a second purchase within the first four weeks following their first purchase, these two cohorts are virtually identical in terms of the (initial) development of repeat buying.

Conclusion

The two different cross-cohort comparisons shown here demonstrate the "art and science" of conducting these sorts of comparisons. Admittedly, neither of these comparisons revealed dramatic

Figure 6.16. Comparing the Cumulative Distribution of Time to Second Purchase for the Q4/2016 and Q4/2017 Cohorts

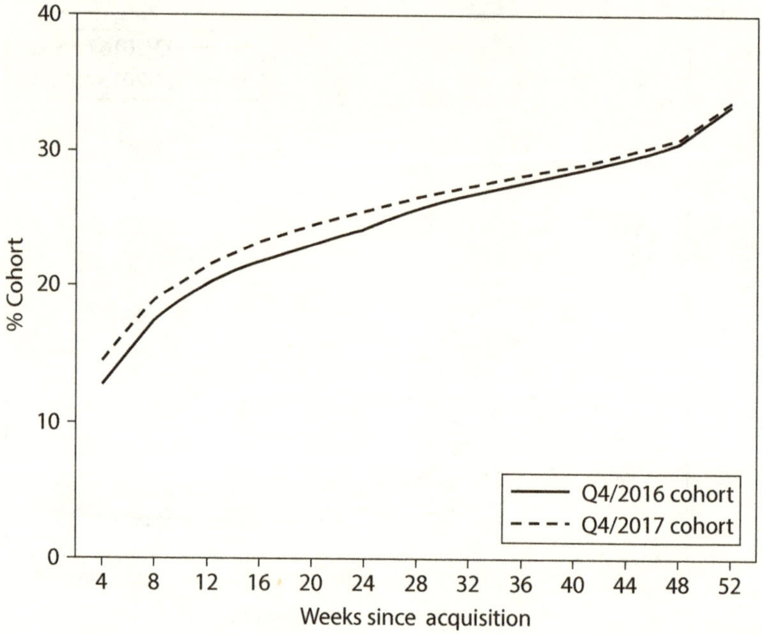

differences, but that is fairly common—and probably a good thing. Cross-cohort stability is generally preferable to seeing wild swings from one group of customers to another that was acquired a few quarters later.

However, these steady numbers should not lull us into a false sense of security. It is important to conduct these kinds of analyses on a regular basis as an early warning sign of degradation in the overall customer base. When cohorts start to get worse (perhaps because the pool of good potential customers has "dried up" or maybe due to competitive activities), the degradation will likely continue—and get worse as time passes. It is important to catch these changes early.

Furthermore, companies that focus purely on aggregate metrics will not see this degradation until after it has occurred for numerous cohorts (perhaps covering two to three years), after which time it has had a visible impact on the customer base as a whole.

Figure 6.17. Comparing the Number of Weeks Taken to Make a Second Purchase for the Q4/2016 and Q4/2017 Cohorts

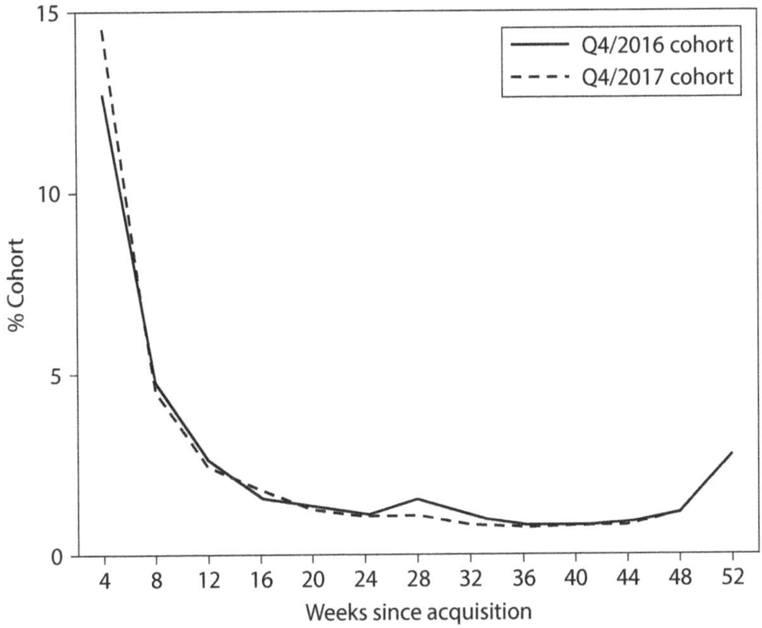

This is why Lens 4 is so important. Like a traditional financial audit, boring is usually good. And where there is smoke, there is often fire.

Executive Questions

- In the same way many companies conduct period-to-period analyses (e.g., same-store sales comparisons), do you conduct cohort-to-cohort analyses as routinely and regularly?
- Beyond a simple aggregate comparison across two cohorts, does your firm have the discipline and analytical skills to "get below the surface" to explain the differences?
- Can you connect the decompositional analysis to marketing (and other) activities to explain why these differences are occurring, and whether they are short-term "blips" or long-term trends?

Chapter 7

How Healthy Is Our Customer Base?

Think back to the data cube introduced in chapter 2 and, in particular, the customer × time face that has been the focus of our discussion thus far. Each chapter has introduced a new way of looking at this face, adding perspectives and complexities not covered in previous ones. We have gone from one to two vertical slices (Lenses 1 and 2), then one to two horizontal slices (cohorts; Lenses 3 and 4). Now it is time to bring everything together. We are finally in a position to answer the ultimate question of a customer-base-audit: From a customer-centric perspective, is Madrigal in "good shape"?

Figure 7.1 reports annual revenue and profit for each of the past four years (this is the same as figure 2.10). While 2017 was not a massive improvement over 2016, seeing a 7% growth in revenue and a 4% growth in profit, 2018 and 2019 were much better. For both years, revenues were up by 21% and profits increased by 18% and 22%, respectively. We should be happy, shouldn't we? Maybe, but maybe not.

How do we diagnose the health of Madrigal in light of what we have learned so far? How do we look at it through the lens of the customer?

We could do a series of Lens 2–type analyses, comparing 2016 with 2017, 2017 with 2018, and so on. However, assuming our database configuration makes it easy for us to identify when each customer was acquired, we can get a better sense of the health of Madrigal's customer base by looking at the evolution of the buying behavior of the various cohorts of customers it has acquired over the

Figure 7.1. Summary of Annual Performance

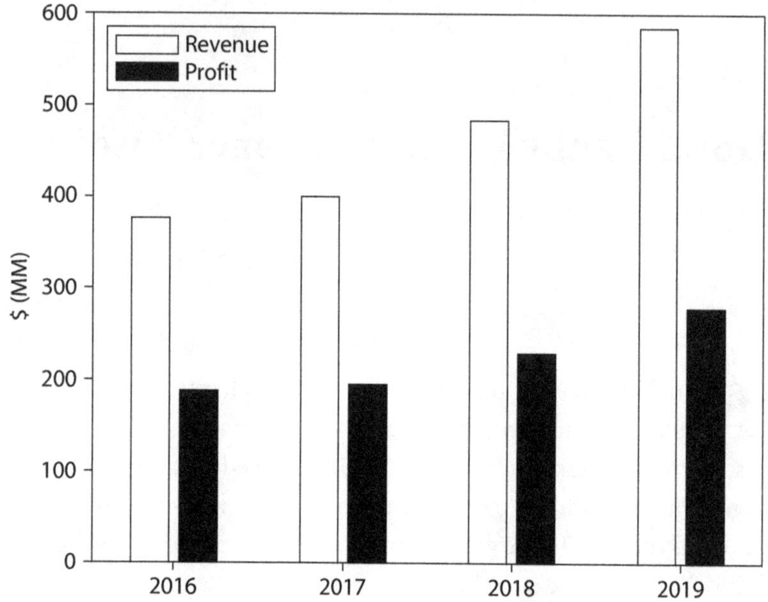

years. Lens 5 sees us extending the ideas developed in our Lens 3 and 4 analyses to the entire customer base.

Understanding the Evolution of Annual Performance

We start by decomposing Madrigal's annual performance by annual cohort (i.e., those customers acquired in a given year). Due to database limitations—unfortunately, not an uncommon problem—we are not able to identify when all of the customers acquired prior to the start of 2016 were actually acquired. We therefore have one "pre-2016" cohort and four annual cohorts (those customers acquired in 2016, 2017, 2018, and 2019).[9] The annual revenue and profit associated with each cohort are reported in table 7.1; figure 7.1 is simply a plot of the total numbers.

We plot the profit numbers in figure 7.2, which shows how much of each year's profits are attributable to customers acquired in that year and in previous years. We can also do this for other quantities—

Table 7.1. Annual Performance by Annual Cohort (in Millions of Dollars)

		2016	2017	2018	2019
Total	Revenue	375.1	399.8	483.5	583.5
	Profit	187.2	195.6	230.2	280.0
pre-2016	Revenue	136.8	111.2	103.1	95.4
	Profit	68.1	54.7	49.4	46.2
2016	Revenue	238.3	92.5	78.8	71.0
	Profit	119.0	44.9	37.3	34.0
2017	Revenue		196.1	73.4	59.8
	Profit		96.0	34.5	28.5
2018	Revenue			228.3	81.8
	Profit			109.0	38.7
2019	Revenue				275.5
	Profit				132.7

such as revenue, active customers, and total orders—but we will focus on profit for now to keep things simple.

What immediately jumps out at us is just how much of each year's profit is due to customers acquired in that year. We also note that a cohort's profit in the year following its formation is much lower than its first-year profit, and it continues to taper off slowly from there. We now examine and expand on each of these observations.

Customer Acquisition

Although we have mentioned customer acquisition several times throughout the book, it has not been a focus of our analysis; a "customer-base audit" tends to center on the assets that a company already has in place. But it is useful (perhaps even vital) to ensure

Figure 7.2. Annual Profit by Year of Acquisition

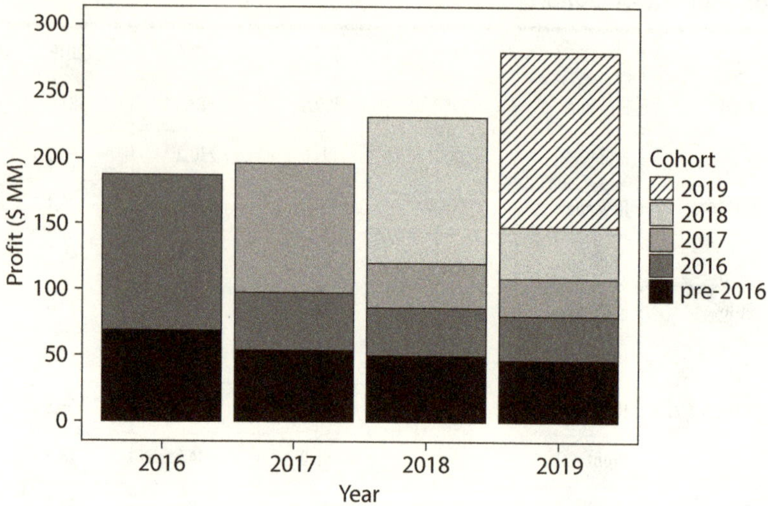

that those assets are continuing to flow into the company in a healthy, sustainable manner. With this in mind, in figure 7.3, we show the annual flow of newly acquired customers.

We note that customer acquisition was down by 15% in 2017, which would account for Madrigal's anemic growth that year. Overall growth resumed for the two subsequent years. Whether or not this represents an ongoing pattern of acquisition growth is an important question, but outside the scope of a customer-base audit.

Back to the Big Picture

With this important piece of the puzzle now in place, we return to the analysis of figure 7.2, sometimes known as a "C3," or "customer cohort chart," a tool that is becoming increasingly popular.[10] In order to address our other observations about it, consider figure 7.4, which is a copy of figure 7.2 with additional detail.

Focusing on the vertical bars associated with each year's profit, the numbers inside each bar are the percentage of that year's profit associated with each cohort. Looking at 2016 (and referring back to

Figure 7.3. Number of Customers Acquired Each Year

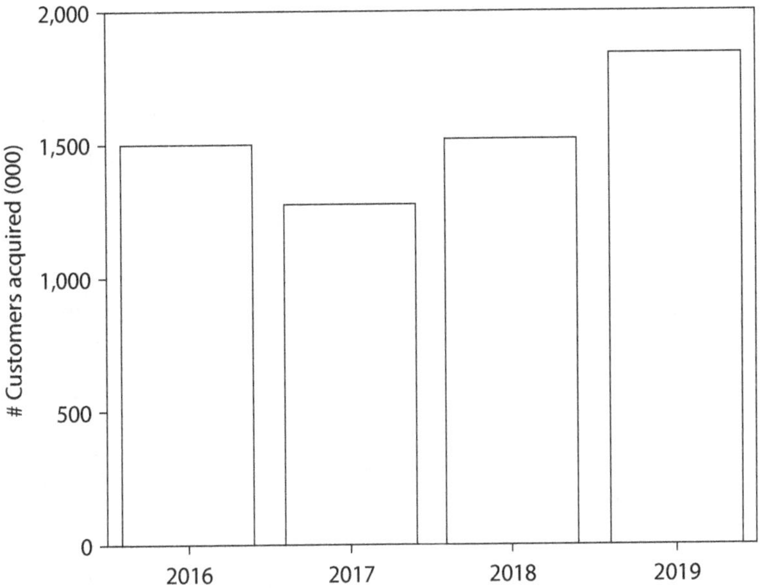

Figure 7.4. Decomposition of Annual Profit by Year of Acquisition

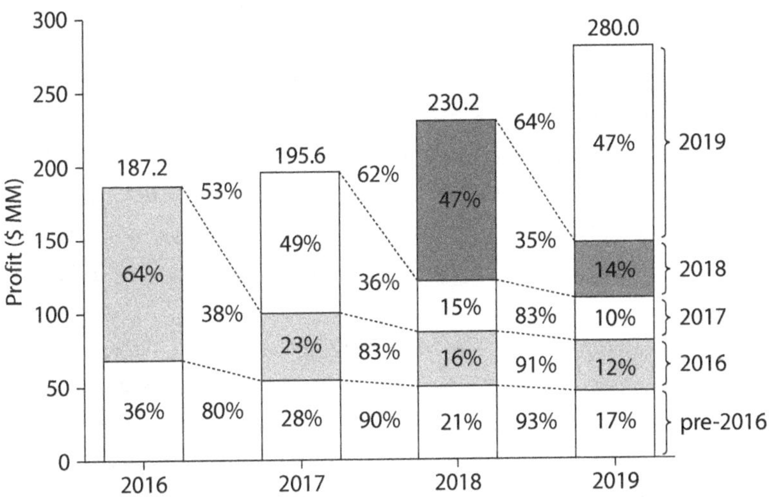

the numbers in table 7.1), we see that 64% (119.0/187.2) of Madrigal's profit that year came from newly acquired customers. Looking at 2019, we see that 47% (132.7/280.0) of Madrigal's profit came from customers acquired that year. Fourteen percent (38.7/280.0) of profit came from customers acquired in the previous year, 10% (28.5/280.0) from customers acquired in 2017, 12% (34.0/280.0) from customers acquired in 2016, and the remaining 17% (46.2/280.0) came from customers acquired before 2016.

Looking from vertical bar to vertical bar, we note how little of any year's profit is "retained" the following year. For example, in 2017, the profit associated with those customers acquired in 2016 and before is just 53% ((54.7 + 44.9)/187.2) of 2016's profit. Similarly, in 2019, the profit associated with those customers acquired in 2018 and before is 64% ((280–132.7)/230.2)) of the profit associated with this group of customers in 2018.

This summary enables us to follow each cohort's profit over time while comparing it to others (a natural extension of Lens 4). Looking at the 2016 cohort profit, we see that the 2017 profit associated with that cohort is 38% (44.9/119.0) of its first-year profit. Its 2018 profit is 83% (37.3/44.9) of its 2017 profit, and its 2019 profit is 91% (34.0/37.3) of its 2018 profit. Looking across all cohorts, we see the largest "loss" of profit is associated with the cohort acquired in the previous year. What lies behind this?

We report in table 7.2 the number of active customers each year by acquisition cohort and the number of transactions they made. We plot the customer numbers in figure 7.5, which shows how much of each year's active customers were acquired in that year and in previous years.

Let us first consider the total number of active customers each year. While 2017 was a minor increase over 2016, with a 4% increase in the size of the active customer base, 2018 and 2019 were much better. In both years, the size of the active customer base grew by 22%. These growth rates are very similar to those observed for the revenue and profit in each year. This implies that Madrigal's revenue and profit growth has been driven mainly by increasing the size of its

Table 7.2. Annual Number of Active Customers and Transactions by Annual Cohort (in 000s)

		2016	2017	2018	2019
Total	Customers	2,063	2,153	2,620	3,185
	Transactions	3,646	4,005	5,106	6,093
pre-2016	Customers	572	467	425	391
	Transactions	1,358	1,137	1,111	1,016
2016	Customers	1,492	413	344	306
	Transactions	2,288	973	879	781
2017	Customers		1,273	335	271
	Transactions		1,895	817	663
2018	Customers			1,517	385
	Transactions			2,299	916
2019	Customers				1,832
	Transactions				2,717

Figure 7.5. Evolution of the Number of Active Customers by Year of Acquisition

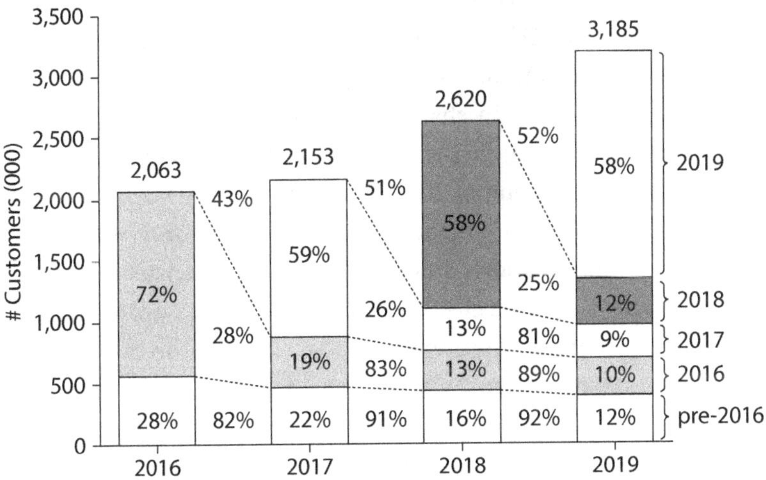

active customer base, as opposed to changes in the value of an active customer. Using the numbers reported in tables 7.1 and 7.2, we can determine that the average annual spend per active customer ranged between $182 and $186 over this four-year period, and the average annual profit per active customer ranged between $88 and $91.

We interpret figure 7.5 in a similar manner to figure 7.4. Looking at 2016, we see that 72% (1,492/2,063) of Madrigal's customers were acquired that year, with the other 28% in an earlier year. Looking at 2019, we see that 58% (1,832/3,185) of its customers were acquired that year, 12% (385/3,185) were acquired in 2018, 9% (271/3,185) were acquired in 2017, 10% (306/3,185) in 2016, and the remaining 12% before 2016.

As an aside, recall our Lens 2 analysis of Madrigal's performance in 2018 and 2019. We noted (chapter 4, figure 4.1) that 2.2 million of the 3.2 million customers active in 2019 had not made a purchase in 2018. We refused to call them "new," because we were not assuming any knowledge of when each customer was acquired. We can now determine that 83% (1,832/2,203) of them were actually new customers acquired that year.

We can also follow a cohort over time. Looking at the 2016 cohort, we see 28% (413/1,492) of the customers Madrigal acquired in 2016 were active in 2017. The number of 2016 cohort members active in 2018 is 83% (344/413) of the number active in 2017, and so on.

We have to be careful when interpreting these cohort-level numbers. Let us elaborate: In chapter 5 we observed that 45% of those customers acquired in the first quarter of 2016 had not made a second purchase by the end of 2019. What are the equivalent numbers for all cohorts? Table 7.3 reports the development of repeat buying for the four annual cohorts. Looking at the row associated with 2017, we see that 27% of those customers acquired in 2017 made a second purchase sometime during that calendar year. By the end of "Year 2" (2018), 41% of those customers had made a second purchase. This means 14% (41–27) of those customers acquired in 2017 made their second-ever purchase sometime during 2018 (these numbers cannot

Table 7.3. Cumulative Percentage of Each Annual Cohort Making Their Second-Ever Purchase

Cohort	Year 1	Year 2	Year 3	Year 4
2016	28%	43%	49%	52%
2017	27%	41%	47%	
2018	27%	40%		
2019	26%			

be determined from table 7.2 alone). While the overall growth pattern is reasonably similar across cohorts, it does appear that members of more recently acquired cohorts are slightly slower to make their second-ever purchase from Madrigal.

Let us reflect on the above observation that 14% of those customers acquired in 2017 made their second-ever purchase with Madrigal sometime in 2018. Looking back at figure 7.5, we note that 26% of the 2017 cohort made at least one purchase in 2018. This means only 46% (1–14/26) of the members of the 2017 cohort active in 2018 were individuals who had made more than one purchase in their year of acquisition.

We also note that the number of 2017 cohort members active in 2019 is 81% of the number active in 2018. This means 26% × 81% = 21% of the 2017 cohort were active in 2019. We see from table 7.3 that 6% (47–41) of the cohort made their second-ever purchase in 2019, which is almost 30% (6/21) of all those members of the 2017 cohort who were active in 2019.

Recall that the number of 2017 customers active in 2019 is 81% of the number active in 2018. We have chosen our words carefully. We did not say that 81% of the 2017 cohort members active in 2018 were active in 2019. The percentage of customers who were active in 2018 that are also active in 2019 is called the repeat-buying rate. We report the repeat-buying rates in table 7.4, both by annual cohort and in the aggregate. As was the case with table 7.3, these numbers cannot be determined from table 7.2 alone.

Let us consider the 2017 row. We see that 26% of those customers who were active in 2017 were also active in 2018; this is also what we see in figure 7.5. Half of those customers from the 2017 cohort who were active in 2018 were also active in 2019 (while some of the other half are "lost," a large proportion are probably reasonably light buyers who may buy again in 2020). This means 62% (50/81) of the 2017 cohort members active in 2019 are customers who were also active in 2018.

Looking at table 7.4 as a whole, we see that the numbers on the "diagonal" are low. These are the same numbers reported in figure 7.5, and we have discussed why they are low. Having "gotten rid of" the one-time buyers, the cohort-level annual repeat-buying rates seem to be reasonably consistent across cohorts. They appear to rise slightly over time toward some steady state; this reflects a "shaking out" of the customer base. The overall repeat-buying rate is simply a weighted average of the repeat-buying rates associated with each cohort, which is why, for any given year, it lies between the repeat-buying rate associated with the most recent cohort and those associated with older cohorts.

Even with these basic numbers, we can do some quick "back of the envelope" calculations that can be of use as we think about

Table 7.4. Annual Repeat-Buying Rates

	2016/17	2017/18	2018/19
pre-2016	52%	56%	57%
2016	28%	51%	54%
2017		26%	50%
2018			25%
Overall	34%	38%	37%

planning for the next year. Let us consider the following example, which is arguably too basic.

With reference to table 7.2 and figure 7.5, we see that Madrigal acquired 1.8 million new customers in 2019, and the remaining 1.4 million customers were acquired in previous years. Let us assume that 25% of those customers acquired in any given year are active the following year. (This is at the lower bound of what we observe in figure 7.5 and table 7.4.) And let us assume that for any older cohort, the number of customers active in one year is 90% of the number active in the previous year. (Looking at figure 7.4, this is probably optimistic.) We can therefore expect to have $0.25 \times 1.8 + 0.9 \times 1.4$, equaling 1.7 million customers next year who come from our existing customer base. If we simply want to stand still in terms of the number of customers, we would have to acquire 1.5 million new customers. If the firm has a target of 20% profit growth (which is approximately what we have observed over the past two years), assuming no change in average annual profit per active customer, we would need about 3.8 million customers in total, or 2.1 million new customers. That is a 16% increase over the number of customers acquired in 2019. Is that achievable?

Digging Deeper

Plots such as figure 7.2 may already be circulating in your firm. However, interpreting them can be a bit difficult since there is no explicit consideration of the size of each cohort. This is why our brief focus on customer acquisition is so important. Not only are the acquisition patterns critical in their own right, but they provide a useful contextual basis for the subsequent cross-cohort comparisons.

Figure 7.4 offers a bit of insight as to how the cohorts differ. However, we can make things much clearer by using the logic of the multiplicative decomposition of cohort performance developed in the previous two chapters.

For each annual cohort, we compute the percentage of the cohort that is active each year and the average profit per active customer. This second quantity is then decomposed into AOF, AOV, and average margin. We present the associated plots of these numbers in figure 7.6.

Figure 7.6a reports the percentage of each annual cohort that is active each year. (Given the data in table 7.2, this is simply the number

Figure 7.6. Decomposing Annual Performance by Cohort

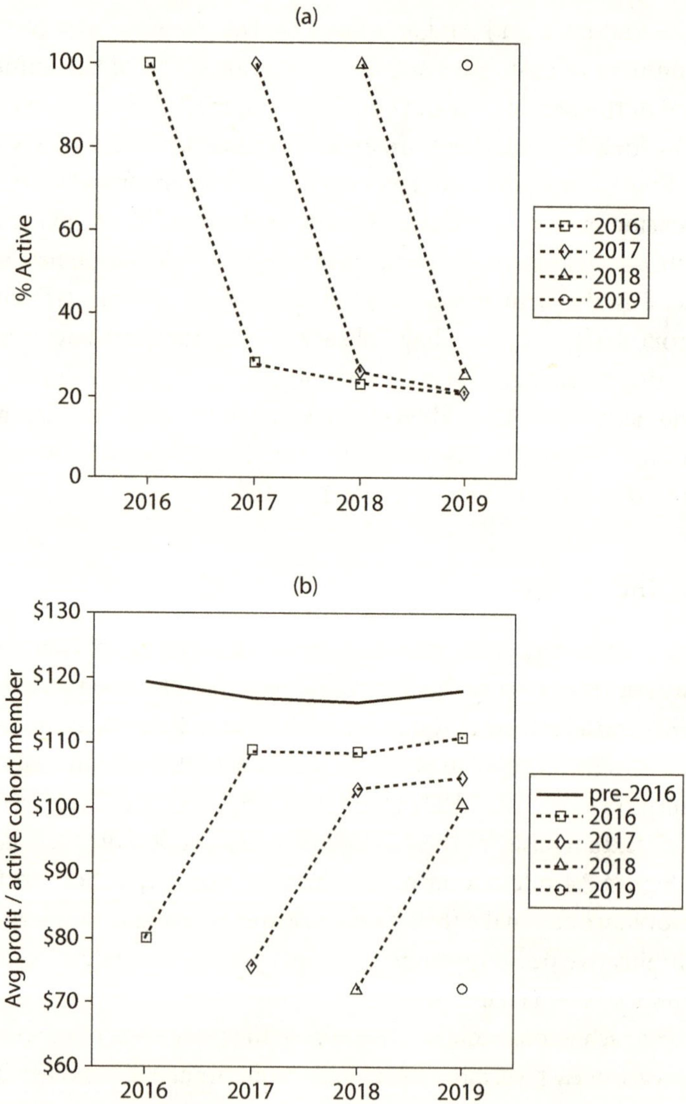

(c)

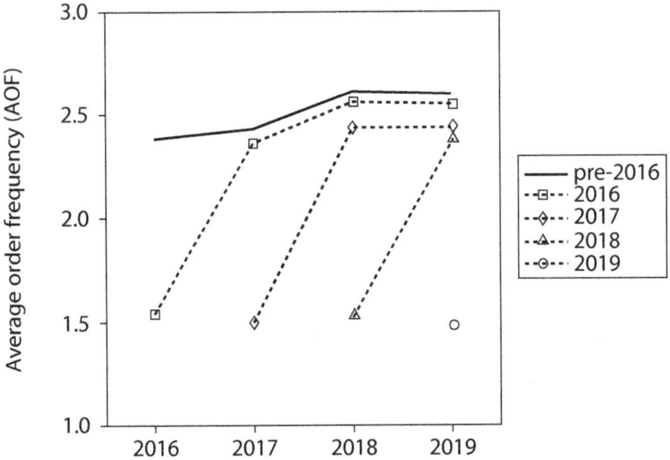

Average order frequency (AOF)
3.0
2.5
2.0
1.5
1.0
2016
2017
2018
2019
pre-2016
2016
2017
2018
2019

(d)

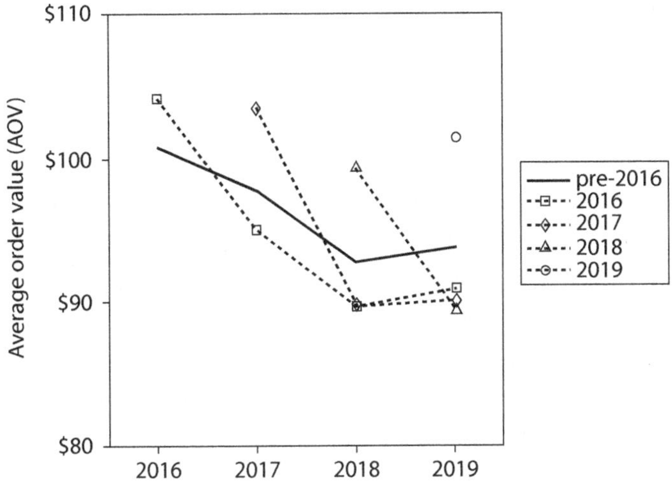

Average order value (AOV)
$110
$100
$90
$80
2016
2017
2018
2019
pre-2016
2016
2017
2018
2019

(e)

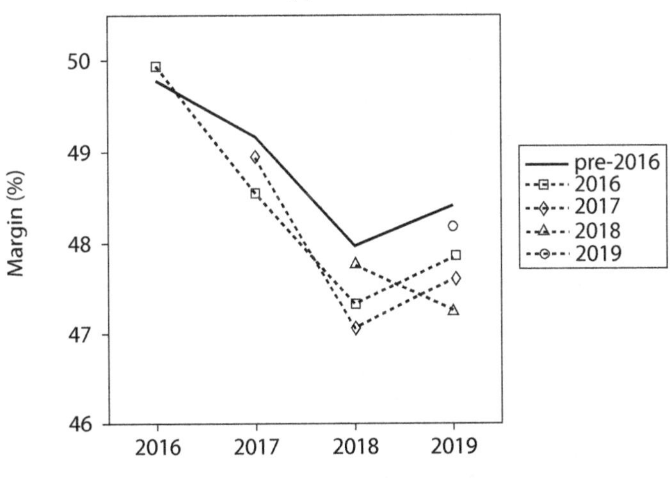

Margin (%)
50
49
48
47
46
2016
2017
2018
2019
pre-2016
2016
2017
2018
2019

of customers from a cohort who are active that year, divided by the size of the cohort.)

The number is obviously 100% in the year that defines acquisition. As already seen in figure 7.5, there is a big drop-off the following year (e.g., only 28% of those customers acquired in 2016 made at least one purchase in 2017). What level of activity do we observe in subsequent years? We see in figure 7.5 that the number of 2016 customers active in 2018 is 83% of the number active in 2017; similarly, the number of 2016 customers active in 2019 is 89% of the number active in 2018. This maps to 23% (28% × 83%) of the 2016 cohort being active in 2018 and 21% (28% × 83% × 89%) being active in 2019, as plotted in figure 7.6a.

We observe that the % active numbers are slowly drifting downward after the initial big drop. While the annual cohorts are not exactly the same, there do not appear to be any major differences between cohorts. By no means is this a general result for all firms, but it is an important pattern to monitor. Note that we do not plot the percentage-active numbers for the pre-2016 cohort, as all we know about these customers is that they were acquired sometime before 2016; we do not know the total number of customers acquired before 2016.

Figure 7.6b reports the average (total annual) profit per buyer for each cohort for each year. Given the data in tables 7.1 and 7.2, this is simply each cohort's annual profit divided by the number of active cohort members that year.

Two things jump out from this plot. The first is that average profit per customer in the first year of a cohort is much lower than the corresponding numbers in subsequent years, about 30% lower on average. Why is this the case?

Recall that average profit per active cohort member is simply AOF × AOV × average margin. These three quantities are reported in figures 7.6c, 7.6d, and 7.6e, respectively.

We see the primary cause of the difference in average profit per active cohort member is the fact that the average number of orders per customer in the year of acquisition is just over 60% of that observed among active members of the cohort in subsequent years.

There are two reasons for this. First, as previously discussed, we have a lot of one-time buyers. Second, as we shall soon see (and as discussed in the previous chapter), a large proportion of each annual cohort's customers are acquired toward the end of each year, which means customers simply have less time in which to make a repeat purchase in that calendar year.

You may recall that the average annual profit per active customer ranged between $88 and $91. How do we reconcile those numbers, which were computed as total annual profit divided by total number of active customers, with what we see in figure 7.6b? Most of the data points in this figure are above $91.

The overall numbers are a weighted average of the cohort-specific numbers. In any given year, the largest proportion of active customers are those acquired that year, and new customers have a lower average profit. This pulls down the overall number. The overall annual average lies between the average profit per active customer associated with that year's cohort and those associated with older cohorts. This is a further illustration of how failing to decompose totals into cohort-level numbers can hide valuable information.

To further illustrate this point, consider the overall annual AOF, AOV, and average margin numbers reported in table 7.5, which are computed using the relevant "total" numbers from tables 7.1 and 7.2. These tend to lie closer to the lower bound of the associated numbers reported in figures 7.6c–7.6e. (Once again, these overall numbers are a weighted average of the cohort-specific numbers.) Looking at these aggregate numbers can be very misleading, masking important differences across cohorts. As such, they should be avoided.

Table 7.5. Overall AOF, AOV, and Average Margin by Year

	2016	2017	2018	2019
AOF	1.8	1.9	1.9	1.9
AOV	$103	$100	$95	$96
Avg margin	50%	49%	48%	48%

The second thing that jumps out from figure 7.6b is that cohort-level average profit per customer appears to be relatively stable beyond the first year. However, unlike what we observed in figure 7.6a, there are noticeable between-cohort differences; active members of the older cohorts are more profitable each year than the active members of the more recently acquired cohorts. With reference to figures 7.6c and 7.6d, this is driven primarily by the inter-cohort differences in both AOF and AOV.

Looking at average margin (figure 7.6e), there would appear to be an overall annual pattern that reflects changes in Madrigal's price and promotional activities. Looking beyond that, we see that customers have a higher average margin in their first year. We also note that, ignoring each cohort's first year, older cohorts have a higher average margin.

Why do we see these inter-cohort differences? We do not have enough information in the raw transaction database to provide an answer to this question. This is where you start having conversations with the relevant people in your firm. Have there been changes in your pricing and promotional policies? Has your product mix changed? And so on. Sometimes there is an obvious explanation, but more often it will be necessary to have discussions focused on these patterns, which may yield various hypotheses that can be explored via additional analyses. This exploration and learning process can be seen as a useful (albeit indirect) benefit of a customer-base audit.

Will you see these same patterns when you look at these same analyses for your firm? There is only one way to find out! The important thing is to do such analyses. A useful exercise is to get a data analyst in your firm to create the equivalent of tables 7.1 and 7.2 for your business. Given those tables, anyone with basic Excel skills can produce all the above analyses except those presented in tables 7.3 and 7.4. This exercise provides very useful insights into the underlying patterns of buyer behavior that lie behind the revenue numbers in your basic financial reports.

As noted above, we can grow our revenues and profits by acquiring new customers. But how can we grow the value of our existing customers? With reference to figure 7.6, it is "simple": increase the percent active in any given year, AOF, AOV, and/or margin (without there being too much of an offsetting decline in the components that do not increase). Of course, that is easier said than done . . . and using promotions to bribe customers to buy from you again is not a good idea. You really need to think about the fundamentals. For any given product (or service) range, what is the potential to get customers to buy from you more often and/or spend more per transaction? Is there much scope to increase your "share of wallet"? In the absence of some underlying shift in (or shock to) consumer behavior, there may be limited scope unless, for instance, you add additional product lines or services (think Amazon). But before we get too carried away with the strategic and tactical implications, let us simply acknowledge that this type of analysis provides focus as you think about business growth and the development of your product/service offerings and marketing activities.

Quarterly Analysis

We have just explored the evolution of Madrigal's annual performance by creating annual cohorts and examining each cohort's annual behavior. Such a high-level analysis is a natural starting point and will be sufficient for many firms implementing a customer-base audit.

However, you are probably used to looking at your firm's quarterly performance, so it is reasonable to think about performing a Lens 5 analysis at that more granular level instead of an annual basis. Figure 7.7 reports Madrigal's quarterly revenue and profit numbers from 2016 to 2019. The thing that jumps out at us, as we have now seen many times, is the marked seasonality in performance; each year, Q4 revenue and profit are more than double the average performance in the previous three quarters.

Given customer visibility, the natural path beyond figure 7.7 would be to decompose Madrigal's quarterly performance as we have done throughout this chapter for annual performance. As a first step

Figure 7.7. Summary of Quarterly Performance

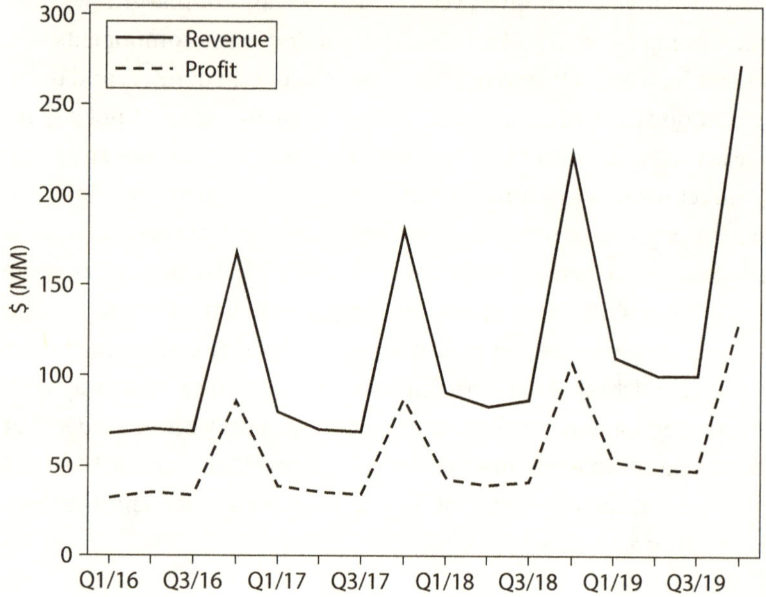

in that direction, we report in figure 7.8 how much of each quarter's profit is attributable to customers acquired in that quarter and in previous quarters. We have 16 quarterly cohorts and one pre-2016 cohort.

We immediately observe that a large proportion of each quarter's profit comes from customers acquired that quarter. This would suggest that a large percentage of each year's new customers are acquired in the fourth quarter. We plot the quarterly flow of newly acquired customers in figure 7.9.

It is quite clear that for Madrigal, Q4 activities (presumably holiday-related marketing) drive acquisitions in a big way. About 45% of the total acquisitions from Q1/2016 through Q4/2019 occur during Q4. Furthermore, the size of the Q4 spike, relative to its immediately preceding quarter(s), appears to be getting larger over time. This could be seen as a "good news/bad news" scenario, in that the Q4 activities seem to be increasingly effective, but the company is becoming more reliant on them. Furthermore, the unique behavior

Figure 7.8. Decomposing Quarterly Profit by (Quarterly) Cohort

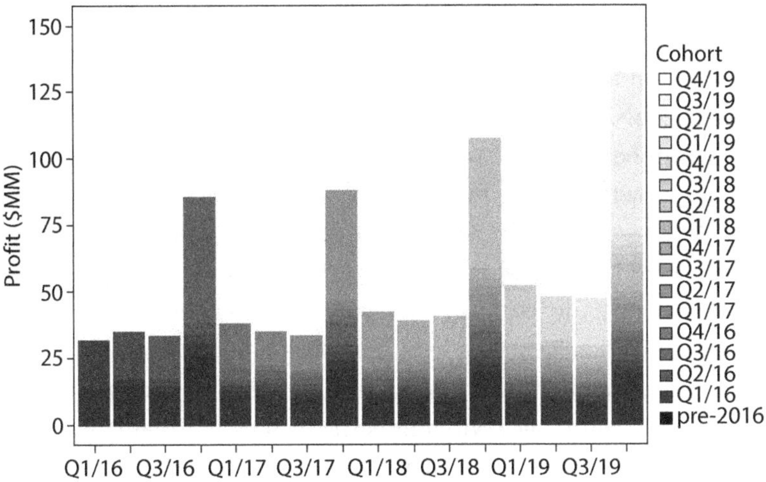

Figure 7.9. Number of Customers Acquired Each Quarter

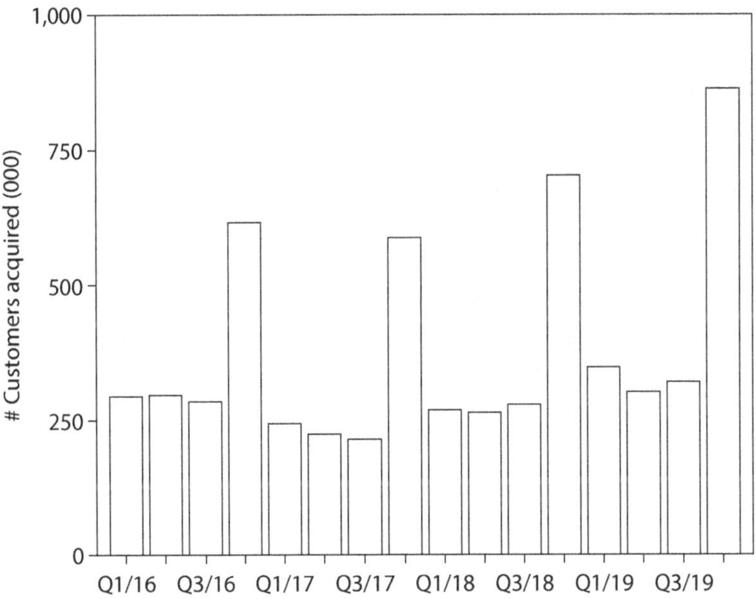

of those Q4 cohorts, as discussed in chapter 6, should be considered as well when judging the quality of these ongoing acquisition strategies and tactics.

Beyond the distinctive Q4 spikes, the baseline pattern for customer acquisition is relatively flat. As observed in the annual acquisition numbers (figure 7.3.), there is a noticeable dip in 2017, but then overall growth resumes for the two subsequent years.

What is almost impossible to determine from figure 7.8 is whether (and, if so how) the cohorts differ from each other. The natural follow-up is to perform the analyses presented earlier in this chapter but at the quarterly level. But we will not present the associated figures and tables because there is an overwhelming amount of detail (and redundancy with our earlier discussions). Furthermore, this more granular analysis may be of limited interest (compared to the annual version) unless you work for Madrigal or are an investor wishing to get more insight into the health of Madrigal as reflected by the health of its customer base.

Conclusion

The title of this chapter asked a question ("How Healthy Is Our Customer Base?") that is, essentially, synonymous with the concept of a customer-base audit. In answering this question throughout the chapter, we have done much of the "heavy lifting" associated with such an audit. For Madrigal we can briefly summarize this assessment using the common framework of acquisition/retention/development:

Acquisition

- After a slight dip in 2017, acquisition has grown steadily in 2018–19. This is obviously a sign of a healthy business.
- But there seems to be more reliance on holiday season (Q4) acquisitions. As discussed earlier, this is a mixed blessing, and it requires a deeper examination of how those quarterly cohorts compare with others.

Retention

- The magnitude of the within-cohort "shakeout" might come as a surprise to many executives, but we see it as quite natural and normal. While many acquired customers seem to fade away after a year or so, enough customers are staying with the company over a longer time frame to suggest that the customer base is staying reasonably strong.
- But some of the repeat-buying behavior (see, e.g., tables 7.3 and 7.4) seems to be slipping a bit across cohorts. This should be closely monitored if the pattern continues, especially if it appears to accelerate.

Development

- Profit levels (as reflected in figures 7.6b–e) seem to be remaining relatively steady over time—a sign of good health. To the extent that there are any dynamics at all, AOF seems to be edging ever so slightly upward (figure 7.6c) for customers who remain active.
- But this same figure also hints at some cross-cohort slippage over time. This is not (yet) a major concern but could become one in the near future.

Overall, this seems to be a reasonably favorable assessment. Perhaps we are putting too much emphasis on the areas of caution, but that is very much in line with the intended spirit of an audit.

Keep in mind this summary is brief—it does not do justice to the full analysis described above and in the previous chapters. Many of the analyses featured in Lenses 1–4, such as decile comparisons, time from one purchase to the next curves, and more can and should be applied across the full set of cohorts as well. A full audit should be a comprehensive endeavor, especially for a firm that is just starting to conduct it on a regular basis. Over time, certain analyses will naturally rise to the top of the priority list, and they will likely vary from one firm to another.

Finally, keep in mind that everything discussed here (and throughout the previous four chapters) has focused exclusively on the customer × time face. The customer-base audit should also cover insights that arise from bringing back the product dimension, which we do in the next chapter.

Executive Questions

- When you get below the purely aggregate accounting metrics (i.e., annual revenue and profit) and into the underlying customer behavior data, what patterns jump out most readily?
- Can you explain these changes in the behavioral indicators? Are they transient or persistent? Can you link them to particular marketing activities?
- Do you see any offsetting trends (e.g., increased AOF but decreasing AOV) that are masked in the aggregate data?
- Have you tried shifting the focal unit of time (e.g., from yearly to quarterly)? What new insights emerge as you move to a more granular level?
- As you perform customer-base audits on an ongoing basis, how do they change as you gain more experience and perspective? Are they simpler or more complex?

Chapter 8

Bringing Back the Product Dimension

The starting point for our journey into the basic set of analyses we associate with the customer-base audit was to note that, at the simplest level, we can characterize a transaction on three dimensions: customer, time, and product. We can therefore conceptualize the firm's transaction database as a cube of data, with the edges representing each of those dimensions.

The reporting systems in most organizations are based on a view of this data cube in which the product × time face is primarily visible, which means we are aggregating over the customer dimension. The main focus of a customer-base audit is to pivot the orientation of the data cube so that the primary focus moves to the customer × time face. This means we are now aggregating over the product dimension.

As we have seen in the last five chapters, this seemingly simple shift in orientation opens up a whole new set of ways to think about your firm's revenues and profits. However, we have been ignoring a rather fundamental reality: The revenue is generated by customers buying the various products and services offered by the firm. So, now that the importance of thinking about a firm's performance through the lens of the customer has (hopefully) been established, let us now bring back the product dimension. Up to now, we have said nothing about the products sold by Madrigal. The firm sells more than 12,000 products, grouped into 23 high-level categories.

We have two goals for this chapter. The first is to explore how the observed customer differences are reflected in the purchasing of products. The second is to explore how our understanding of product performance can be enhanced by taking advantage of knowledge of the customer dimension.

Understanding Customer Differences in One Period

Chapter 3 introduced the first lens by which we can examine customer behavior, exploring how customers differ in their spend, number of transactions, and profitability. A capstone analysis that brought together a number of the ideas developed in that chapter was the profit-based decile analysis. We present in table 8.1 a slightly edited version of the original table.

Each decile represents a group of customers whose profit in 2019 was 10% of Madrigal's profit that year. For each decile, the average profit per customer is the product of average order frequency (AOF), average order value (AOV), and average margin. While there are

Table 8.1. Summary of the 2019 Customer Profit-Based Deciles

Decile	% Customers	Avg profit per cust	AOF	AOV	Avg Margin
1	1%	$843	10.9	$156	50%
2	2%	$433	6.3	$138	50%
3	3%	$300	4.6	$132	50%
4	4%	$223	3.6	$125	50%
5	5%	$171	2.9	$119	49%
6	7%	$132	2.4	$113	49%
7	9%	$102	2.0	$106	49%
8	11%	$77	1.7	$96	48%
9	17%	$52	1.5	$77	47%
10	41%	$21	1.2	$45	41%

some differences in margin, the key drivers of the differences in average profit per customer are the differences in AOF and AOV.

What lies behind these differences? We present in table 8.2 a high-level summary of the category buying behavior of the members of each decile.

Let us first consider the customers' breadth of buying. For each customer we determine the number of categories in which they made at least one purchase during 2019, along with the number of unique SKUs they purchased. We report the averages of these two quantities by decile.

Not surprisingly, the higher-value customers are buying in more categories and purchasing a broader range of products throughout the year. How is this reflected in their transaction-by-transaction behavior? Why do higher-value customers have a higher AOV? Is the broader range of products purchased over the year reflected in the

Table 8.2. Summary of Product Purchasing by Decile

Decile	Avg # categories	Avg # unique SKUs	Avg # units/ transaction	Avg price/ unit	Avg # units/ category	Avg # categories/ transaction
1	5.8	33.8	3.6	$44	2.3	1.6
2	4.5	18.2	3.2	$44	2.0	1.5
3	3.8	12.6	3.0	$44	2.0	1.5
4	3.3	9.6	2.9	$44	1.9	1.5
5	2.9	7.5	2.7	$44	1.8	1.5
6	2.5	5.8	2.6	$43	1.8	1.5
7	2.2	4.6	2.5	$43	1.7	1.4
8	1.9	3.7	2.3	$41	1.7	1.4
9	1.7	3.0	2.2	$36	1.6	1.4
10	1.3	1.9	1.7	$26	1.4	1.2
	2.0	4.3	2.4	$39	1.7	1.4

individual transactions, or is it reflected more by the fact that the higher-value customers make more transactions with Madrigal throughout the year and therefore have a chance to purchase from a broader range of product categories?

To explore this, let us consider a simple multiplicative decomposition of AOV:

$$\begin{aligned} \text{AOV} &= \frac{\text{revenue}}{\#\,\text{transactions}} \\ &= \frac{\text{revenue}}{\#\,\text{units}} \times \frac{\#\,\text{units}}{\#\,\text{transactions}} \\ &= \begin{matrix}\text{average price}\\ \text{per unit}\end{matrix} \times \begin{matrix}\text{average \# units}\\ \text{per transaction}\end{matrix} \end{aligned}$$

Looking at these two quantities in table 8.2, we see that for the top-five deciles (the 15% of customers who accounted for half of Madrigal's profit in 2019), there is no variation in average price per unit (when rounded to the nearest dollar). Therefore, the differences in AOV are due to the differences in the number of units purchased per transaction.

You might be wondering whether we should compute an average price per unit when we are averaging across categories where the average price of a product will vary across categories. To what extent do any observed differences in average price per unit reflect differences in the mix of product categories purchased? This is a valid concern. We should investigate variations in the mix of products purchased and explore the extent to which this is driving observed differences in average price per unit. This is too much detail for the high-level analyses we would associate with a customer-base audit but is an obvious "next step" analysis that an analyst within the firm should undertake.

Are these differences in the average number of units per transaction a result of the customers buying more units in a given category (be it more unique products or more units of the same product) or buying in more categories on any given transaction? To explore this, let us consider a simple multiplicative decomposition of the average number of units per transaction:

$$
\begin{aligned}
\begin{matrix}\text{average \# units}\\ \text{per transaction}\end{matrix} &= \frac{\text{\# units}}{\text{\# transactions}} \\
&= \frac{\text{\# units}}{\text{\# categories purchased}} \times \frac{\text{\# categories purchased}}{\text{\# transactions}} \\
&= \begin{matrix}\text{average \# units}\\ \text{per category}\end{matrix} \times \begin{matrix}\text{average \# categories}\\ \text{per transaction}\end{matrix}
\end{aligned}
$$

A quick aside on the number of categories purchased measure: If customer A made two transactions with the firm in the period of interest, buying in categories X and Y on their first purchase occasion and category X on their second purchase occasion, and customer B made one transaction with the firm, buying in category Z, the number of categories purchased across the three (firm-level) transactions by these two customers is four.

Looking at table 8.2, we see that both quantities (average number of units per category and average number of categories per transaction) are higher for the more profitable deciles. However, we see a greater variation in the former (from 1.4 to 2.3) than the latter (1.2 to 1.6). Because there is little variation in the average number of categories purchased in any given transaction, the higher average number of categories purchased in 2019 by the higher-value deciles goes hand in hand with their higher AOF (table 8.1).

Madrigal's higher-value customers buy more often and spend more per transaction. This higher spend per transaction is primarily driven by the fact that they have more items in their average basket. This is principally due to their buying more items in a given category rather than more categories in a given transaction. The higher number of categories and unique SKUs they buy over the course of the year reflects the fact that they have more transactions with Madrigal in 2019.

Exploring Category Performance Given Customer Visibility

Table 8.3 lists the 23 product categories sold by Madrigal, providing information on the number of products and SKUs associated with each category, the category-level 2019 revenue and profit, and each category's share of Madrigal's 2019 profit. The categories are sorted by 2019 profit. Note that the category names have been changed to disguise the source of the data.

The top four categories, which represent just under 70% of Madrigal's 2019 profit, contain just under 62% of the products and 73% of the SKUs stocked.

Given customer visibility, we can also look at SKU, product, and category performance via the lens of the customers, using many of the types of analyses we have considered at the firm level. For example, a useful way to understand category performance is to make use of the now-familiar multiplicative decomposition of revenue and profit. However, there is an important difference in this setting: In the previous chapters, we were decomposing *firm-level* profit; now we want to look at *category-level* performance. It is therefore important that we make the distinction between a customer's purchasing in a given category and their transactions with the firm. (The former is obviously less than or equal to the latter.)

We can decompose category profit (for a given period) as:

$$\begin{aligned}\text{category profit} &= \#\,\text{category buyers} \times \frac{\text{category profit}}{\#\,\text{category buyers}} \\ &= \#\,\text{category buyers} \times \begin{array}{c}\text{average category profit}\\ \text{per category buyer}\end{array}\end{aligned}$$

For any given period, the number of category buyers will be a subset of the number of customers that made at least one purchase from the firm:

Table 8.3. Summary of Category Performance in 2019

Category	# SKUs	# Products	Revenue ($MM)	Profit ($MM)	Share of profit
Men's sportswear	45,346	1,784	$124.9	$61.7	22.0%
Women's sportswear	52,291	4,364	$115.5	$57.9	20.7%
Women's fashion	11,812	884	$88.1	$43.8	15.6%
Men's fashion	4,528	454	$66.6	$31.4	11.2%
Men's accessories	11,936	970	$40.1	$18.8	6.7%
Women's accessories	14,641	1,178	$33.9	$15.1	5.4%
Women's shoes	3,160	218	$19.7	$9.1	3.3%
Men's shoes	1,942	183	$14.8	$6.6	2.4%
Jewelry	568	187	$14.5	$6.4	2.3%
Gifts	658	322	$10.0	$4.3	1.5%
Food	2,189	132	$10.9	$4.1	1.5%
Sports	970	238	$7.5	$3.8	1.4%
Watches	1,145	67	$9.8	$3.7	1.3%
Toys	972	315	$5.8	$3.0	1.1%
DIY	55	18	$2.7	$2.2	0.8%
Kids' fashion	314	73	$4.2	$1.8	0.6%
Kids' shoes	451	199	$4.1	$1.6	0.6%
Technology	321	117	$2.6	$1.2	0.4%
Beauty	521	155	$2.2	$1.1	0.4%
Home	604	201	$2.2	$1.1	0.4%
Garden	282	34	$1.5	$0.7	0.3%
Baby	238	19	$0.9	$0.3	0.1%
Bags	437	30	$1.0	$0.3	0.1%
Total	155,381	12,142	$583.5	$280.0	100.0%

$$\#\text{category buyers} = \#\text{active firm customers} \times \frac{\#\text{category buyers}}{\#\text{active firm customers}}$$

$$= \#\text{active firm customers} \times \begin{array}{c}\%\text{ customers active}\\ \text{in the category}\end{array}$$

Recalling the decompositions from previous chapters, we can decompose average category profit per category buyer as:

$$\begin{array}{c}\text{average category profit}\\ \text{per category buyer}\end{array} = \frac{\text{category profit}}{\#\text{category buyers}}$$

$$= \frac{\#\text{category transactions}}{\#\text{category buyers}} \times \frac{\#\text{category revenue}}{\#\text{category transactions}} \times \frac{\#\text{category profit}}{\#\text{category revenue}}$$

$$= \begin{array}{c}\text{average } \textit{category}\\ \text{order frequency}\end{array} \times \begin{array}{c}\text{average } \textit{category}\\ \text{order value}\end{array} \times \begin{array}{c}\text{average } \textit{category}\\ \text{margin}\end{array}$$

Pulling these together, we have category profit = the number of active firm customers (in the given period of time) × the percentage of customers active in the category (which we will also call category penetration) × average *category* order frequency (ACOF) × average *category* order value (ACOV) × average *category* margin.

It is important to make the distinction between ACOF and ACOV, and AOF and AOV. The former are category-level quantities; the latter are firm-level quantities.

Given the 3.2 million active Madrigal customers in 2019, table 8.4 reports the components of this decomposition for each category.

The two categories that represent the highest share of Madrigal's 2019 profits are the two categories with the highest penetration (or percentage of 2019 customers that made at least one purchase in the category during the year). The two categories have very similar ACOF and ACOV; the men's sportswear category's slightly higher share of Madrigal's 2019 profits relative to the women's sportswear category

Table 8.4. Decomposition of Category Performance

Category	% Active in category	ACOF	ACOV	Avg cat margin	Avg # units/order	Avg price/ unit
Men's sportswear	33.2%	1.6	$75	50%	2.1	$36
Women's sportswear	29.5%	1.7	$74	50%	2.1	$36
Women's fashion	16.6%	1.3	$131	50%	1.2	$113
Men's fashion	13.1%	1.2	$130	47%	1.1	$114
Men's accessories	15.0%	1.4	$58	47%	2.2	$26
Women's accessories	14.5%	1.5	$49	45%	2.1	$23
Women's shoes	6.1%	1.2	$86	46%	1.1	$75
Men's shoes	5.0%	1.1	$82	44%	1.2	$71
Jewelry	7.3%	1.2	$52	44%	1.4	$37
Gifts	7.8%	1.3	$32	42%	1.7	$19
Food	3.7%	1.2	$78	37%	1.1	$68
Sports	7.1%	1.2	$28	51%	1.4	$19
Watches	3.3%	1.2	$82	38%	1.1	$74
Toys	6.0%	1.2	$25	51%	1.5	$17
DIY	9.6%	1.2	$7	81%	1.1	$7
Kids' fashion	3.9%	1.2	$29	42%	1.3	$22
Kids' shoes	5.4%	1.2	$20	39%	1.8	$11
Technology	0.5%	1.2	$138	47%	1.5	$90
Beauty	2.9%	1.1	$21	49%	1.4	$15
Home	3.0%	1.2	$20	49%	1.5	$13
Garden	0.4%	1.1	$92	44%	1.3	$69
Baby	0.7%	1.1	$37	34%	1.1	$35
Bags	0.8%	1.1	$36	33%	1.1	$33

is down to the former category's slightly higher penetration of the active customer base (33.3% versus 29.5%).

We also report in table 8.4 a decomposition of ACOV into average number of units per category order × average price per unit. While there is some variation in the average number of units purchased per category order, the biggest driver of ACOV is, not surprisingly, the average price of a SKU in each category.

Some other useful measures of customers' category buying behavior are presented in table 8.5.

We first look at the percentage of Madrigal's 2019 customers that only purchased in the focal category that year, which we call "% sole category buyers." We see that almost 14% of Madrigal's 3.2 million customers only purchased from the men's sportswear category. Recalling from table 8.4 that the penetration of this category is just under a third of the customer base, we can express this another way: For 41% (13.7/33.2) of those customers, all their 2019 purchasing with Madrigal was from this category. For Madrigal, this quantity is highly correlated with category penetration: The higher the category penetration, the greater the proportion of category buyers that only buy from that category.

Note that the sum of this column is 53%. That means 53% of Madrigal's 2019 customers only purchased from one category that year. (When reflecting on this number, remember from chapter 3 that 63% of the 2019 customers made only one transaction with Madrigal.) Next, we look at the average number of categories purchased by those customers that made at least one purchase in the focal category. For example, we see in table 8.5 that, on average, those customers that made at least one purchase in the men's sportswear category purchased in a total of 2.4 categories. Generally speaking, those customers that bought products in the lower-penetration categories purchased in more categories.

Another quantity of interest is the (average) percentage of a customer's total firm-level profit that comes from the focal category. For example, for those customers that made at least one purchase in the men's sportswear category, almost half of their profit came from their

Table 8.5. Additional Measures of Category Buying Behavior

Category	% Sole cat buyers	Avg # categories	Cat share of cat buyers' profit	Most common additonal category	% Buying
Men's sportswear	13.7%	2.4	49%	Women's sportswear	27%
Women's sportswear	10.0%	2.6	47%	Men's sportswear	30%
Women's fashion	5.9%	2.7	49%	Women's sportswear	37%
Men's fashion	4.9%	2.6	46%	Men's sportswear	38%
Men's accessories	3.9%	3.0	38%	Women's accessories	37%
Women's accessories	2.9%	3.2	32%	Men's accessories	38%
Women's shoes	1.2%	3.5	35%	Women's accessories	50%
Men's shoes	0.9%	3.5	31%	Men's accessories	51%
Jewelry	2.4%	3.0	20%	Women's sportswear	32%
Gifts	1.3%	3.5	11%	Men's sportswear	45%
Food	0.9%	3.5	19%	Women's sportswear	50%
Sports	1.0%	3.5	10%	Men's sportswear	55%
Watches	1.0%	3.2	21%	Men's sportswear	47%
Toys	0.7%	3.7	9%	Women's sportswear	56%
DIY	0.3%	3.5	5%	Men's sportswear	40%
Kids' fashion	0.5%	3.9	13%	Women's accessories	46%
Kids' shoes	0.5%	3.9	8%	Women's accessories	48%
Technology	0.2%	2.9	35%	Women's sportswear	32%
Beauty	0.2%	4.3	8%	Men's accessories	61%
Home	0.2%	4.4	8%	Women's accessories	61%
Garden	0.2%	3.0	27%	Women's sportswear	28%
Baby	0.1%	4.5	10%	Men's accessories	60%
Bags	0.1%	4.7	9%	Women's accessories	64%

purchases in that category; the same holds for the next three categories in table 8.5. The magnitude of this quantity is generally negatively correlated with the average number of categories purchased and positively correlated with the ACOV for that category.

Overall, we see that the categories for which a high percentage of a customer's total profit comes from that category are higher-penetration categories. Of course, there are exceptions, including a notable one: The technology category was purchased by only 0.5% of Madrigal's 2019 customers (table 8.4), yet it accounted for 35% of the total profit of those purchasers (table 8.5). Some of this will be attributable to the fact that this category has the highest ACOV (table 8.4).

The final bit of analysis we will consider here looks at the co-purchasing of various categories. For each category, we compute the percentage of category buyers that made at least one purchase in each of the other categories. Rather than report a table with 23 rows and 23 columns, we report in table 8.5 the category most frequently purchased by the buyers of the focal category, along with the percentage of the focal category buyers who purchased that category. For example, 27% of those customers who made at least one purchase in the men's sportswear category also made at least one purchase in the women's sportswear category. Generally speaking, the most common additional category is one of the two categories purchased by the largest proportion of the 2019 customer base (i.e., men's sportswear or women's sportswear).

Recall from our discussion of table 8.2 that Madrigal's higher-value customers buy more often and spend more per transaction. This higher spend per transaction is primarily driven by the fact that they have more items in their average basket. This is largely a result of their buying more items in a given category rather than purchasing from more categories on a given transaction. What was missing from our discussion, though, was how this was manifested in the customers' purchasing of different categories. To explore this, let us compare the behavior of decile 1 customers to that of all Madrigal's 2019 customers.

We present in table 8.6 the category profit per customer for the average Madrigal customer and the average decile 1 customer.

Table 8.6. Average Profit per Customer and Category Share of Profit for All Customers and Decile 1 Customers

Category	Profit per customer			Category share of profit		
	All	Decile 1	Index	All	Decile 1	Index
Men's sportswear	$19	$180	930	22.1%	21.4%	97
Women's sportswear	$18	$248	1367	20.7%	29.5%	142
Women's fashion	$14	$140	1021	15.6%	16.6%	106
Men's fashion	$10	$99	1002	11.2%	11.7%	104
Men's accessories	$6	$25	430	6.7%	3.0%	45
Women's accessories	$5	$27	576	5.4%	3.2%	60
Women's shoes	$3	$12	422	3.3%	1.4%	44
Men's shoes	$2	$9	454	2.3%	1.1%	47
Jewelry	$2	$20	1019	2.3%	2.4%	106
Gifts	$1	$13	947	1.5%	1.5%	99
Food	$1	$13	1031	1.5%	1.6%	107
Sports	$1	$12	973	1.4%	1.4%	101
Watches	$1	$10	903	1.3%	1.2%	94
Toys	$1	$9	1004	1.1%	1.1%	105
DIY	$1	$9	1285	0.8%	1.0%	134
Kids' fashion	$1	$2	348	0.6%	0.2%	36
Kids' shoes	$1	$2	458	0.6%	0.3%	48
Technology	$0	$5	1278	0.4%	0.6%	133
Beauty	$0	$2	470	0.4%	0.2%	49
Home	$0	$2	517	0.4%	0.2%	54
Garden	$0	$1	685	0.2%	0.2%	71
Baby	$0	$0	410	0.1%	0.0%	43
Bags	$0	$1	510	0.1%	0.1%	53
Total	$88	$843	959	100.0%	100.0%	

Note that the denominator is the total number of customers, not just the number buying in each category. In other words, the "All" profit per customer numbers are simply the respective category profit numbers reported in table 8.3 divided by 3.2 million, the total number of Madrigal customers in 2019. The index is simply 100 × decile 1 profit / All profit. A value of 100 indicates that the two quantities are the same. We also report each category's share of firm profit and decile 1 profit, along with the associated index.

The average decile 1 customer is worth $843, 9.6 times that of an average 2019 Madrigal customer, whose profit is $88. As such, the profitability per category is much higher, but this is not distributed equally across categories. For example, we see that the profit of an average decile 1 customer attributed to the women's sportswear category is over 13 times that of an average customer, while the profit attributable to the kids' fashion category is only 3.5 times higher. As a result, almost 30% ($248/$843) of the decile 1 customers' profit comes from the women's sportswear category, compared to just over 20% ($18/$88) for the average customer.

What lies behind these differences in profitability associated with each category? Is it because a greater proportion of customers buy in some categories? Or is it because buyers of those categories buy them more often during the year? Spend more per transaction? Buy higher-margin products?

To answer such questions, we report in table 8.7 the quantities reported for all 2019 buyers in table 8.4 just for decile 1 customers. Note that the profit per customer numbers reported in table 8.6 are the product of the % active, ACOF, ACOV, and average category margin numbers.

The category margins associated with the purchasing of decile 1 customers are basically the same as those associated with the overall Madrigal customer base (as shown in table 8.4). This means the observed differences in profit are due to differences in category penetration, ACOF, and/or ACOV.

Table 8.7. Decomposition of Category Performance for Decile 1

Category	% Active in category	ACOF	ACOV	Avg cat margin	Avg # units/order	Avg price/unit
Men's sportswear	70.9%	4.8	$105	50%	2.7	$38
Women's sportswear	77.1%	5.8	$108	52%	2.9	$38
Women's fashion	63.3%	2.6	$171	51%	1.5	$117
Men's fashion	48.1%	2.3	$185	48%	1.5	$124
Men's accessories	20.8%	3.3	$78	47%	2.9	$27
Women's accessories	22.3%	3.7	$71	46%	2.9	$25
Women's shoes	13.6%	2.0	$98	47%	1.4	$71
Men's shoes	11.1%	1.8	$106	44%	1.5	$71
Jewelry	29.0%	1.8	$89	44%	2.2	$41
Gifts	35.1%	2.0	$41	43%	1.9	$21
Food	23.1%	1.7	$87	39%	1.3	$69
Sports	36.9%	1.9	$33	51%	1.6	$20
Watches	17.6%	1.6	$94	39%	1.2	$77
Toys	34.8%	1.9	$28	51%	1.7	$17
DIY	28.1%	2.1	$19	82%	1.2	$15
Kids' fashion	8.5%	1.6	$34	41%	1.5	$23
Kids' shoes	11.8%	2.0	$26	39%	1.9	$13
Technology	3.9%	1.5	$184	47%	1.9	$95
Beauty	8.4%	1.7	$23	49%	1.6	$14
Home	9.0%	1.7	$23	49%	1.8	$13
Garden	2.4%	1.4	$101	43%	1.6	$63
Baby	2.4%	1.2	$39	35%	1.1	$36
Bags	2.9%	1.4	$41	33%	1.2	$35

Comparing table 8.7 with table 8.4, it turns out that the increase in average profit is associated with increases in all these quantities, primarily driven by more people buying the category, followed by an increase in the average number of times customers buy in the category. On average, category penetration is 3.6 times higher, ACOF is 1.7 times higher, and ACOV is 1.3 times higher. Two noticeable exceptions are the men's sportswear and women's sportswear categories, where the increases in ACOF are higher than the increases in penetration: 3 (4.8/1.6) and 3.4 (5.8/1.7) times higher, respectively, for ACOF versus 2.1 (70.9/33.2) and 2.6 (77.1/29.5) times higher for penetration. It follows from these higher penetration numbers that, on average, decile 1 customers purchased from more categories during 2019 (table 8.2).

Reflecting on decile 1's higher ACOV numbers for all categories, is this because they are buying more expensive items, or because they are buying greater quantities whenever they make a category purchase? The last two columns of table 8.7 present the multiplicative decomposition of ACOV. Comparing them to the equivalent numbers in table 8.4, we observe that it is driven primarily by an increase in the average number of items purchased per category purchase. Across all categories, the average increase in average units/order is 21% in contrast to an average 8% increase in average price/unit.

Understanding Customer Differences in Product Purchasing over Time

We have explored differences in customer profitability in 2019 by exploring how the profit deciles differed in terms of their buying of the product categories.

Chapter 5 introduced the third lens by which we explored how the behavior of a cohort of customers evolves over time. A capstone analysis was a profit-based decile analysis of the cohort members' value to date (VTD), which is their cumulative profit from time of acquisition to the end of 2019. We replicate the associated summary table in table 8.8.

Table 8.8. Summary of Q1/2016 Cohort Behavior by VTD Decile

Decile	% VTD	% Cohort	% Trans	Avg VTD	AOF	AOV	Margin
1	10%	1%	7%	$2,441	36.3	$136	50%
2	10%	1%	8%	$1,247	20.5	$123	49%
3	10%	2%	8%	$842	14.6	$117	49%
4	10%	3%	9%	$609	11.1	$111	49%
5	10%	4%	9%	$451	8.6	$107	49%
6	10%	5%	9%	$334	6.6	$103	49%
7	10%	7%	10%	$243	5.0	$99	49%
8	10%	10%	10%	$168	3.7	$94	48%
9	10%	16%	11%	$105	2.5	$89	48%
10	10%	51%	20%	$34	1.4	$59	40%
				$171	3.7	$97	48%

While we could repeat much of the above analyses in this setting, we will focus on some new analyses that give us insight into the evolution of the customers buying in different categories over time.

We report in table 8.9 the cumulative number of unique categories in which members of each decile purchased over time. Looking at the row associated with the first decile, we see that, on average, members of decile 1 had purchased in 4.9 different categories by the end of their first year as a customer of Madrigal. By the end of 2017, this had increased to 6.9 different categories. After four years as customers of Madrigal, they had made purchases in nine different categories.

How should we interpret these numbers? Do they mean decile 1 customers are buying a broader range of products each year? Furthermore, why do we see such a small increase in the number of categories purchased by decile 10 customers? To what extent is this

Table 8.9. Cumulative Average Number of Categories Ever Purchased by VTD Decile

Decile	2016	2017	2018	2019
1	4.9	6.9	8.2	9.0
2	4.0	5.6	6.8	7.6
3	3.4	4.7	5.8	6.5
4	3.1	4.1	5.0	5.6
5	2.8	3.7	4.4	4.9
6	2.5	3.2	3.8	4.2
7	2.3	2.8	3.3	3.6
8	2.1	2.4	2.7	3.0
9	1.8	2.0	2.2	2.3
10	1.4	1.5	1.5	1.6

due to the fact that only 5% of the cohort members associated with that decile make any purchase in 2019 (table 5.2)?

In table 8.10, we report the average number of unique categories purchased each year, conditional on the individual customer being active that year. What jumps out is the surprising stability over time for each decile. Looking at the row associated with decile 1, it is not the case that the number of categories in which the average customer buys in each year increases over time; they are making purchases in approximately five different categories each year. But the set of categories in which they buy varies across the years, leading to a growing number of categories in which they have ever made a purchase (table 8.9). The same pattern (albeit with lower numbers) holds for every other decile as well.

Less profitable customers buy fewer categories, but the dynamics over time are quite similar to those of more profitable customers.

As is the case with every finding described here, it is hard to say whether this is a generalizable result. But at least in this case, it has

Table 8.10. Average Number of Unique Categories Purchased per Year Among Active Customers by VTD Decile

Decile	2016	2017	2018	2019
1	4.9	5.2	5.3	4.9
2	4.0	4.0	4.0	3.9
3	3.4	3.3	3.3	3.3
4	3.1	2.8	2.9	2.9
5	2.8	2.5	2.6	2.6
6	2.5	2.2	2.3	2.4
7	2.3	2.0	2.1	2.1
8	2.1	1.8	1.9	1.9
9	1.8	1.6	1.7	1.7
10	1.4	1.4	1.5	1.5

strong implications for the role and impact of cross-selling activities; it does not appear that customers are truly broadening their relationships with Madrigal over time; they are simply jumping in and out of different categories (if they are active at all).

How is the development of category buying spread across the 23 categories Madrigal sells? In table 8.11, we report the percentage of decile 1 customers that have made at least one purchase in each category by the end of each of the four years under consideration.

If we look at the growth over the four-year period, we see the lowest growth rate for the two highest-penetration categories. By the end of 2016, 64% of decile 1 customers have made at least one purchase in the men's sportswear category, and 73% of the decile 1 customers have made at least one purchase in the women's sportswear category. By the end of 2019, this has increased by 31% to 84% (31% = (84 − 64)/64) for men's sportswear and by 22% to 89% (22% = (89 − 73)/73) for women's sportswear. We see greater growth for those categories purchased by fewer customers in 2016. It would

Table 8.11. Cumulative Penetration of Categories by Decile 1 of Q1/2016 Cohort

Category	2016	2017	2018	2019
Men's sportswear	64%	76%	81%	84%
Women's sportswear	73%	83%	87%	89%
Women's fashion	53%	68%	76%	80%
Men's fashion	37%	51%	60%	65%
Men's accessories	20%	27%	32%	35%
Women's accessories	23%	31%	36%	39%
Women's shoes	13%	18%	22%	24%
Men's shoes	9%	14%	17%	20%
Jewelry	27%	42%	53%	57%
Gifts	27%	43%	54%	60%
Food	20%	33%	41%	47%
Sports	25%	39%	50%	57%
Watches	13%	22%	28%	33%
Toys	27%	43%	53%	60%
DIY	14%	30%	44%	50%
Kids' fashion	8%	12%	15%	18%
Kids' shoes	10%	16%	20%	23%
Technology	2%	4%	5%	7%
Beauty	6%	11%	14%	17%
Home	9%	14%	17%	20%
Garden	3%	4%	5%	6%
Baby	2%	3%	5%	6%
Bags	1%	4%	6%	6%

appear that as customers expand the repertoire of categories from which they purchase over time (table 8.9), they are drawing from a broader range of product categories.

Exploring Category Purchasing and VTD

Finally, let us look at categories through the lens of customer acquisition and subsequent value, in particular VTD (value to date). As we will see in our concluding chapter, in which we show you how to put customer-base audit concepts into action, this sort of analysis is hugely important.

With reference to table 8.12, we first report total spend by the members in the Q1/2016 cohort over the four-year period. (The sum of this column is $50.5 million, the total VTD of this cohort, as noted in chapter 5.) The top four categories among this cohort of buyers are the same as those observed for all 2019 customers (table 8.3), albeit with a swapping in the order of the top two categories.

Next, we consider how many members of the cohort ever purchased in the category over the four-year period, which we express as the percentage of the cohort ever buying in the category ("% Ever buying cat"). With the exception of DIY, these numbers are all higher than the 2019 category penetration rates ("% Active in category") reported in table 8.4. (On average, they are 43% higher.) This should not come as a surprise, as 58% of the customers active in 2019 were acquired in 2019 (figure 7.5), and they have not had much time to explore the range of categories sold by Madrigal. In contrast, members of the Q1/2016 cohort have had a long time to do so (as reflected in table 8.9).

Which categories do people tend to buy on their first-ever transaction with Madrigal? For each category, we report the percentage of the cohort buying in the category on their first transaction ("% Buying cat on first trans").

Looking at the ratio of these two numbers gives us the percentage of the cohort ever buying in the category that did so on their first purchase transaction with Madrigal. Not surprisingly, the categories

Table 8.12. Category Purchasing and VTD for the Q4/2016 Cohort

Category	Category 4-yr profit ($MM)	% Ever buying cat	% Buying cat on first trans	% Ever-buyers buying cat on first trans	For buyers of cat on first trans		
					Tot VTD ($MM)	Avg VTD	Index
Men's sportswear	$11.1	38.2%	25.6%	66.9%	$14.0	$185	108
Women's sportswear	$12.6	38.4%	25.3%	65.7%	$16.2	$218	127
Women's fashion	$7.5	23.0%	13.4%	58.5%	$9.4	$238	139
Men's fashion	$4.0	15.4%	8.4%	54.4%	$5.4	$219	128
Men's accessories	$3.3	20.6%	12.4%	60.4%	$5.1	$141	82
Women's accessories	$3.5	22.0%	13.8%	62.8%	$6.1	$150	88
Women's shoes	$1.6	10.5%	5.3%	51.2%	$2.6	$164	95
Men's shoes	$1.0	7.5%	3.8%	50.1%	$1.8	$158	92
Jewelry	$1.2	10.4%	4.5%	43.4%	$2.6	$197	115
Gifts	$0.6	10.0%	3.2%	32.0%	$1.7	$183	107
Food	$0.7	5.4%	1.8%	34.2%	$1.2	$230	134
Sports	$0.5	9.0%	3.3%	37.1%	$1.9	$197	115
Watches	$0.5	3.8%	1.2%	31.2%	$0.8	$220	128
Toys	$0.5	8.3%	2.9%	34.3%	$2.0	$235	137
DIY	$0.5	9.4%	2.9%	31.0%	$1.8	$207	121
Kids' fashion	$0.3	6.1%	2.5%	40.8%	$1.0	$138	81
Kids' shoes	$0.3	8.3%	3.3%	39.2%	$1.3	$131	76
Technology	$0.2	0.9%	0.5%	55.7%	$0.2	$177	103
Beauty	$0.2	4.7%	1.8%	38.0%	$0.8	$147	86
Home	$0.2	6.1%	2.8%	45.1%	$1.3	$157	91
Garden	$0.1	0.9%	0.5%	53.7%	$0.3	$192	112
Baby	$0.0	0.8%	0.1%	8.9%	$0.0	$147	86
Bags	$0.0	0.9%	0.0%	0.6%	$0.0	$94	55

that tend to appear in a customer's first transaction are the larger categories, albeit with some variation. For example, men's and women's accessories are the fifth and sixth most profitable categories, both for this cohort and in 2019 (table 8.3). However, their likelihood of appearing in a customer's first transaction is higher than that for men's and women's fashion (the third and fourth most profitable categories).

When a smaller category appears in a high proportion of first-time purchases, it is natural to ask whether it is an important category for attracting customers, especially higher-value customers. As a first step in exploring this, we can compute for each category the total VTD (across all categories) for those members of the cohort that purchased from the category on their first-ever transaction with Madrigal. Dividing this by the number of customers that purchased from that category on their first transaction gives us the average VTD for those customers. Recalling from chapter 5 that the average VTD of a member of the Q1/2016 cohort is $171, we can create an index to get a sense of whether, on average, those customers buying in the category on their first transaction are more valuable customers.

Looking at the women's fashion row, we see that the total VTD of the 13.4% of the 294,450 individuals in the Q1/2016 cohort who purchased from this category on their first transaction is $9.4 million. This corresponds to an average VTD of $238, which is 39% higher than that of an average cohort member (index = 139 = 238/171). This could suggest that this category is important for attracting higher-value customers.

The natural follow-up is to perform such analyses by VTD decile and product subcategory. However, we will not present the associated tables because they would contain an overwhelming amount of detail and they would be of limited interest unless you work for Madrigal.

Conclusion

This chapter had two objectives: First, to go a level deeper into the customer-base audit by understanding how differences across products reflect aspects of customer behavior that would be overlooked by focusing purely on the customer × time face of the data cube. Second, we aimed to bring new perspectives about products—from a customer-centric lens—that usefully complement the traditional product-centric view.

For an organization that already has a pretty good grip on its customer-level data (and the behavioral patterns associated with it), the analyses performed here might be seen as "icing on the cake" for the audit—more of a "nice to know" than a "must-have" compared to the coverage in the previous chapters. But for the many organizations that are in a less sophisticated position regarding their understanding of the behavior of their customer base, the analyses laid out here might actually be an effective starting point to help nudge them to view products differently and to actively embrace customer data to better understand how products impact firm performance through the keystone linkage of customer behavior.

As a specific example, consider the customer profitability data in table 8.6 vis-à-vis the overall product profitability data in table 8.3 for the two largest categories: Men's sportswear is a more profitable category than women's sportswear ($61.7 million versus $57.9 million). But decile 1 customers who buy women's sportswear have been 38% more profitable, on average, for Madrigal than buyers of men's sportswear ($248 versus $180). From a product management standpoint, the implications of this kind of analysis are clear and important. Products should be seen as a vital conduit of customer profitability, but ultimately it is the customer driving revenue, not the product.

Another important insight from this brief comparison is a reminder that not all customers are created equal. Note that the comparison made above only covers decile 1 customers, so for less-valuable customers, men's sportswear must be associated with greater profitability than women's sportswear. This points out the strategic trade-off that all companies should acknowledge: Do they want to focus on developing/promoting products associated with more (but less valuable) customers, or focus more on products that help distinguish (and perhaps attract) the best customers? A thorough customer-base audit—with careful consideration of product-level information—is essential when making this kind of decision.

Finally, we acknowledge an important limitation of the analyses covered here: They are all conducted at the category level. We did this for simplicity, but this high level of aggregation likely "smooths over" some stronger patterns that may exist at the product level. Differences among the 1,784 products in the men's sportswear category (table 8.3) may be even more polarizing (i.e., they discriminate between high- and low-value customers) than differences across categories. Customers generally buy *products*, not *categories*, so important aspects of their behavior will be better seen at that level.

Executive Questions

- Do you regularly examine your product sales data with visibility into the customer level? Do you understand who is buying what?
- Before contemplating a full audit, what kinds of basic analyses do you perform with this integrated dataset? What are the first "crossover" (product × customer) questions you seek to answer?
- Do you seek to know which products tend to be disproportionately favored by high-value customers?
- Do you use decompositional analyses to understand what behavioral aspects (e.g., frequency, order size) are most strongly associated with these differences?
- Do your product-focused managers (e.g., in R&D, planning, merchandising) ever ask these questions (or leverage their answers) to help make or evaluate their decisions?

Chapter 9

Variations on a Theme

The last six chapters have seen us identifying a set of analyses we consider to be fundamental to a customer-base audit using data from a retailer we call Madrigal as a running example. As we noted in chapter 2, we realize most readers of this book are not working in the retail sector. However, in our experience, when it comes to the types of analyses one can undertake to understand customer behavior, the differences between business settings are not as big as they may seem. We have developed and fine-tuned many of the types of analyses discussed here in numerous nonretail businesses. We hope that as you have read through this book, you have been able to identify how the analyses would need to be adapted (if at all) for your specific business setting.

In this chapter, we reflect on some of the key changes or additional analyses that may be required in other settings.

Contractual Settings

From a customer-base audit perspective, what is the fundamental difference between your relationship with your local coffee shop and your electric utility? If you no longer want to be a customer of the coffee shop, what do you do? Absolutely nothing. On the other hand, if you no longer want the services of your electric utility, you have to contact them and cancel your contract. From the company's perspective, the loss of a customer is unobserved by the coffee shop. Does the lack of purchasing mean you are "dead" or just on vacation? There is no such uncertainty on the part of your electricity supplier. They know when you "die" as a customer.

We use the terms "noncontractual" and "contractual" to describe such business settings. Madrigal is obviously operating in a noncontractual setting. In certain sectors, it is more common to use the term "subscription" than contractual, but we see them as identical for our purposes here. The past decade has seen a growth in the number of firms built around a subscription model. "Software as a service" (SaaS) has become ubiquitous in both consumer and business computing, and terms such as "membership economy" have become aspirational for many firms (and entire sectors) that have not traditionally viewed their customer relationships in such a manner.

The extent to which the analyses developed in previous chapters apply in a contractual setting depends on the exact nature of the business being considered. If revenue associated with a subscription is known up front, as is the case for a magazine with a single one-year subscription option, customers will not differ in their value in a given year, and the Lens 1 analysis, which focuses on differences in buying behavior in a given period of time, will be of no value. Every customer (under a given subscription plan) is worth the same amount. Maybe the magazine offers three subscription options, with different prices for one-, two-, or three-year subscriptions. Or it offers a print-only, digital-only, and print-plus-digital option. This does result in some between-customer differences in value, but they often are not sufficiently interesting to warrant a set of Lens 1 analyses.

In some situations, revenue associated with the contract or subscription is not fully known in advance. The basic subscription provides access to the product or service, but the customer's revenue per period will depend on their activities while under contract. One simple example is a gym where members pay for additional classes. Another is a SaaS setting in which business customers buy different numbers of "seat licenses." When the customer revenue per period is not known in advance, it will be useful to undertake a set of Lens 1 analyses.

This logic can be extended to a "pure" subscription model for which the company cares about usage of the service, even if there is no direct revenue from the customer arising from it. For instance, a digital magazine might want to track media consumption levels for various reasons. In this case, a Lens 1 analysis of usage would make sense—and the patterns will often look remarkably similar to those discussed in chapter 3.

If the nature of the contractual setting is such that a Lens 1 analysis is warranted, we can also undertake a Lens 2 analysis. However, it is fair to say that, for contractual settings, the cohort-based analyses presented in Lenses 3 through 5 will lie at the heart of any customer-base audit. How similar they are in the contractual setting will depend on what lies behind the revenue per contract period, as discussed above.

Let us consider how these cohort-based analyses change in a contractual setting. Recall from our analysis of Madrigal's customers that the profit associated with a cohort in a given period was decomposed as cohort size × % active customers × average profit per active customer. It makes sense to talk about the percentage of the cohort that is active. It may take a number of periods for a customer to make their second purchase with the firm, and the fact that a customer does not make a purchase in one period does not mean they are "dead" as a customer. Recall, for example, the seasonality observed in the quarterly % active plots examined in chapters 5 and 6.

In a contractual setting, a customer either renews their contract at the end of the specified period, or they do not. We then know how many members of a cohort are still "alive," and we can talk about the number of cohort members that have "survived" as customers over time.

Let us consider a hypothetical example of a firm operating in a contractual setting that acquired 10,000 customers at the beginning of Period 1. We report in table 9.1 the number of cohort members who still have a contractual relationship with the firm in each of the subsequent 15 periods; depending on your business setting, this could be a week, month, quarter, or year.

Table 9.1. Number of Cohort Members Surviving over Time

Period	# Cust (000)	Period	# Cust (000)
1	10.0	9	2.4
2	6.5	10	2.2
3	5.0	11	2.1
4	4.1	12	1.9
5	3.5	13	1.8
6	3.1	14	1.7
7	2.8	15	1.7
8	2.6	16	1.6

The equivalent of the % active plots considered in chapters 5–7 is the survival curve plot given in figure 9.1, which simply reports the numbers in table 9.1 as a percentage of the size of the cohort.

One important thing to note about the survival curve is that it is monotonically decreasing. It cannot increase. If a customer is lost, they are lost. Should they take out another contract at a later date, they are generally considered to be a member of that new cohort.[11]

A long-established metric used in contractual settings is the *retention rate*, or its complement, the *churn rate*. The retention rate is the ratio of the number of customers that renewed their contract (or did not cancel) to the number of customers "at risk" (i.e., could have canceled/not renewed) at a given point in time. This quantity can be computed at the level of the cohort or at the firm level.

With reference to table 9.1, the Period 1 retention rate is the proportion of customers at risk at the end of Period 1 that remain as customers in Period 2: 6.5/10.0 = 0.65. Similarly, the Period 2 retention rate is the proportion of customers at risk at the end of Period 2 that remain as customers in Period 3: 5.0/6.5 = 0.77. And so on. These numbers are plotted in figure 9.2. When computed at the level of the cohort, retention rates typically increase with the tenure or "age" of the cohort (as observed here).

Figure 9.1. Cohort-Level Survival Curve

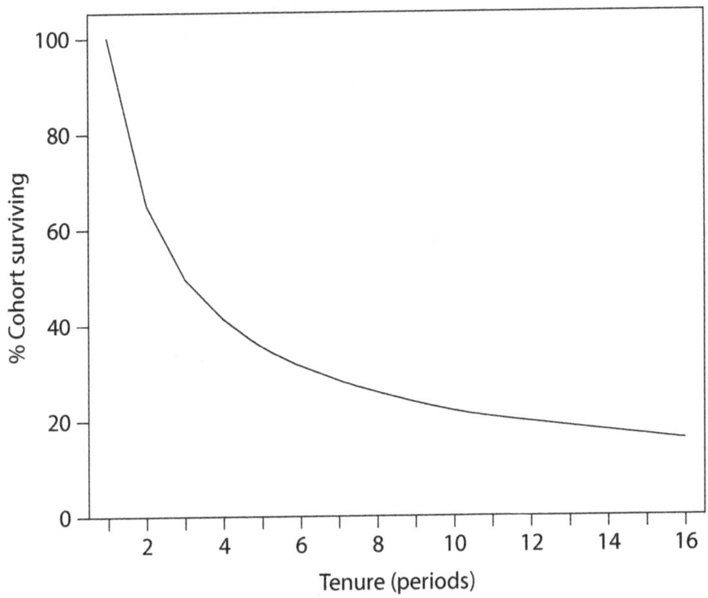

Figure 9.2. Cohort-Level Retention Rate Curve

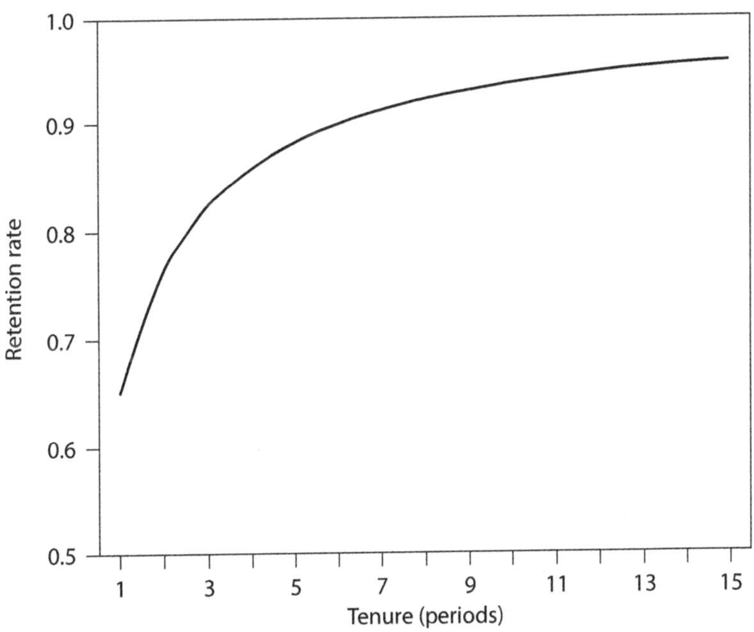

Continuing our toy example, suppose we observe the firm for 16 periods. Each period, it acquires 10,000 customers, whose survival pattern is exactly the same from cohort to cohort (i.e., that given in table 9.1). The evolution of the number of customers the firm has, broken down by cohort, is given in table 9.2 and plotted in figure 9.3.

In figure 9.2, we plotted the cohort-level retention rate. The retention rate may also be computed at the level of the firm. It is simply the ratio of the number of customers that renewed their contract (regardless of whether they were acquired last period or many periods earlier) to the number of customers "at risk" (again, with no conditioning on when they were acquired).

With reference to table 9.2, the aggregate retention rate for Period 1 is computed in the following manner. In Period 2, the firm had 16,500 customers, but only 6,500 (16,500–10,000) were survivors from the previous period. The retention rate is therefore 0.65. In Period 3, the firm had 21,500 customers, but only 11,500 (21,500–10,000) were customers in Period 2. The Period 2 retention rate is therefore 11.5/16.5 = 0.70. And so on. The associated aggregate (i.e., firm-level, as opposed to cohort-level) retention rate is plotted in figure 9.4a.

At first glance, it may seem similar to the curve shown in figure 9.2, but it is a misleading comparison. It does not represent the retention pattern for any cohort, but rather an "apples and oranges" blend across cohorts of different vintages.

To make this clear, consider figure 9.4b, which overlays the cohort-specific retention rate curves. Each cohort had the same retention rate evolution, and the aggregate retention rate slowly grows as the core of the firm's customer base gets older. In and of itself, the aggregate retention curve is not that useful because it gives us no insight into cohort-level behavior. Furthermore, as we will illustrate, it is strongly influenced by the nature of the customer acquisition pattern (which, of course, has nothing to do with retention, per se).

Looking back at table 9.2, the bottom row gives us the size of the firm's customer base each period. Recall that the firm is adding 10,000 customers each period. After an early growth spurt, the annual

Table 9.2. Development of the Firm's Customer Base

		Period												
		1	2	3	4	5	6	7	8	...	13	14	15	16
Cohort	1	10.0	6.5	5.0	4.1	3.5	3.1	2.8	2.6	...	1.8	1.7	1.7	1.6
	2		10.0	6.5	5.0	4.1	3.5	3.1	2.8	...	1.9	1.8	1.7	1.7
	3			10.0	6.5	5.0	4.1	3.5	3.1	...	2.1	1.9	1.8	1.7
	4				10.0	6.5	5.0	4.1	3.5	...	2.2	2.1	1.9	1.8
	5					10.0	6.5	5.0	4.1	...	2.4	2.2	2.1	1.9
	6						10.0	6.5	5.0	...	2.6	2.4	2.2	2.1
	7							10.0	6.5	...	2.8	2.6	2.4	2.2
	8								10.0	...	3.1	2.8	2.6	2.4
	⋮										⋮	⋮	⋮	⋮
	13										10.0	6.5	5.0	4.1
	14											10.0	6.5	5.0
	15												10.0	6.5
	16													10.0
	Total	10.0	16.5	21.5	25.6	29.1	32.3	35.1	37.6	...	48.0	49.8	51.4	53.0

Figure 9.3. Growth in the Size of the Subscriber Base Broken Down by Cohort

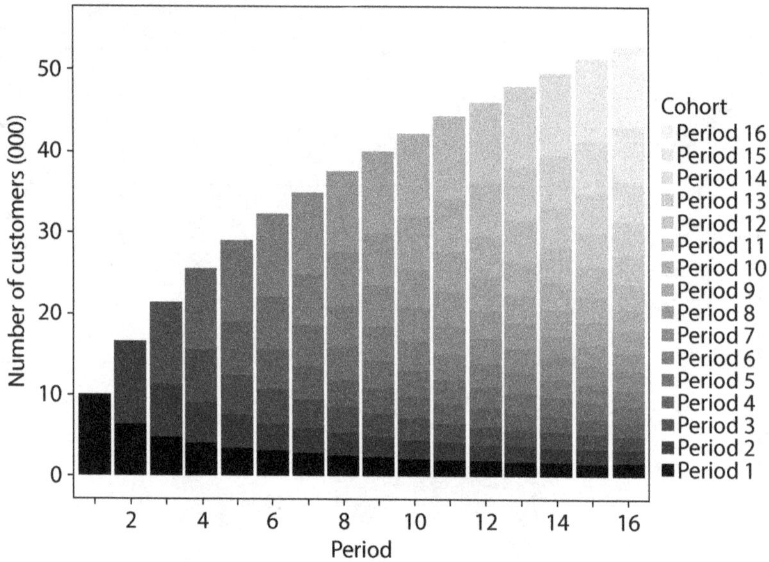

growth rate levels off quickly. By Period 16, period-by-period growth in the size of the firm's customer base is 3%. Projecting out the pattern in figure 9.3, the size of the customer base will keep growing but at an ever-decreasing rate. More and more, it is the case that the newly acquired customers are simply replacing those lost from previous periods.

This toy example has considered a setting where the same number of customers are acquired each period. Let us consider an alternative toy example in which the firm acquires 5,000 customers in Period 1 and the number of customers acquired each period grows by 20% each period. However, the survival and retention pattern for each cohort is the same (figures 9.1 and 9.2). The evolution of the number of customers the firm has is given in table 9.3 and plotted in figure 9.5.

With reference to figure 9.5, the size of the firm's customer base is growing exponentially over time.

Figure 9.4. (a) Aggregate Retention Rate and (b) Compared to Cohort-Specific Retention Rates

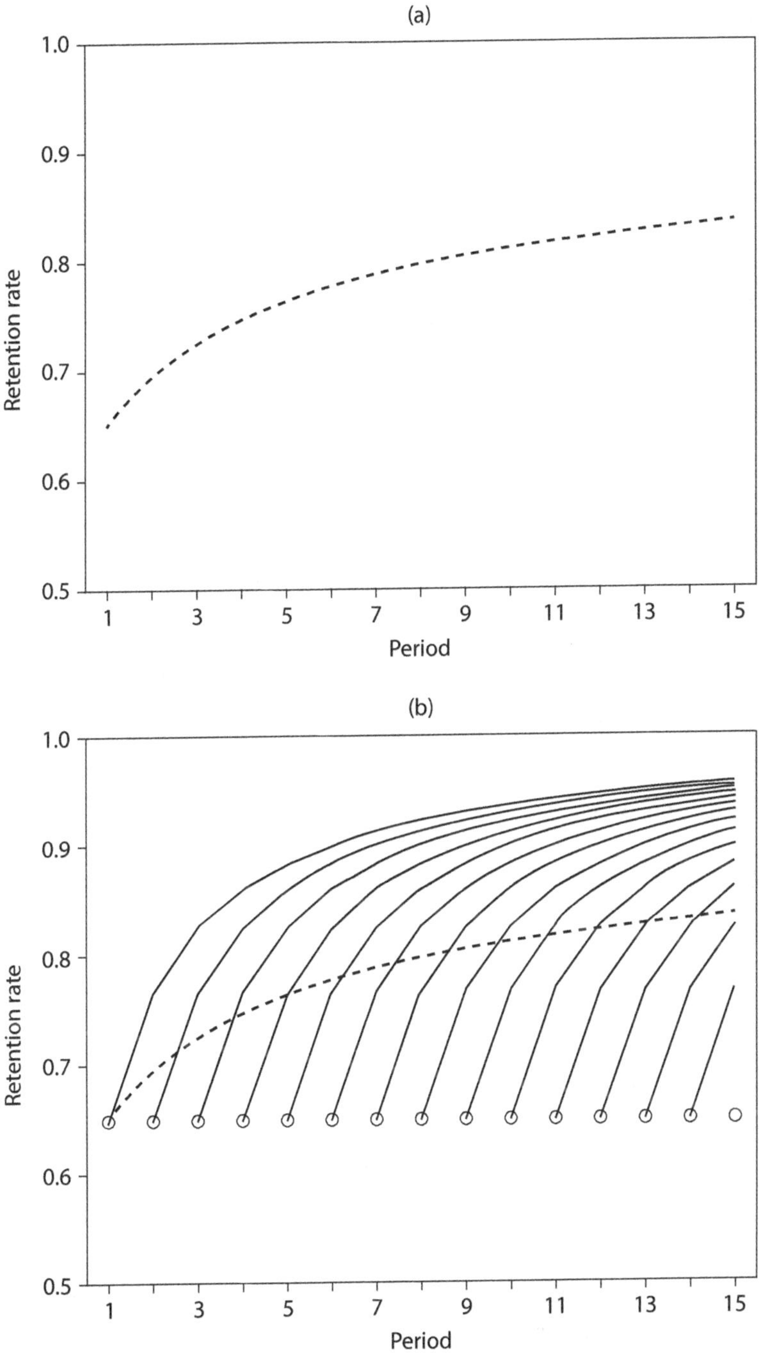

Table 9.3. Development of the Firm's Customer Base

		Period												
		1	2	3	4	5	6	7	8	...	13	14	15	16
Cohort	1	5.0	3.3	2.5	2.1	1.8	1.6	1.4	1.3	...	0.9	0.9	0.8	0.8
	2		6.0	3.9	3.0	2.5	2.1	1.9	1.7	...	1.2	1.1	1.0	1.0
	3			7.2	4.7	3.6	3.0	2.5	2.2	...	1.5	1.4	1.3	1.3
	4				8.6	5.6	4.3	3.6	3.1	...	1.9	1.8	1.7	1.6
	5					10.4	6.7	5.2	4.3	...	2.5	2.3	2.1	2.0
	6						12.4	8.1	6.2	...	3.2	2.9	2.7	2.6
	7							14.9	9.7	...	4.2	3.8	3.5	3.3
	8								17.9	...	5.6	5.0	4.6	4.2
	⋮										⋮	⋮	⋮	⋮
	13										44.6	29.0	22.2	18.3
	14											53.5	34.8	26.7
	15												64.2	41.7
	16													77.0
	Total	5.0	9.3	13.6	18.4	23.8	30.1	37.6	46.4	...	123.3	148.8	179.4	216.0

Figure 9.5. Growth in the Size of the Subscriber Base Broken Down by Cohort

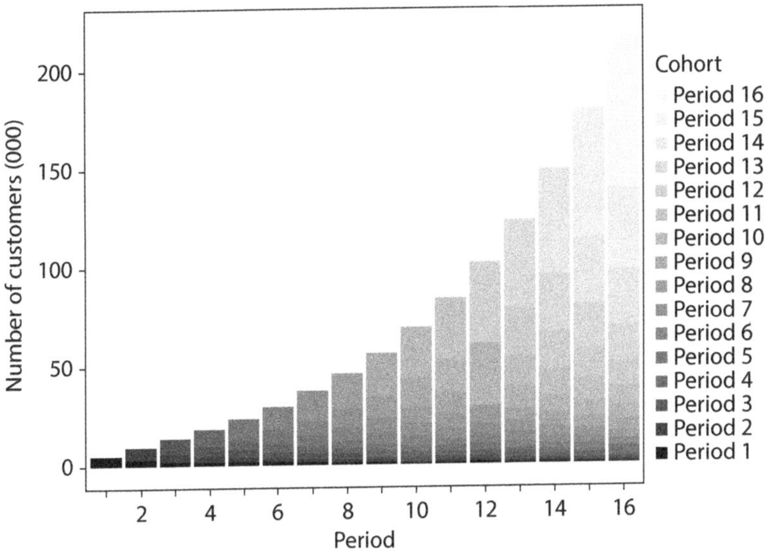

We compute the aggregate retention rate for each period and plot it in figure 9.6 along with the aggregate retention rate from figure 9.4. The aggregate retention rate for the growing acquisition scenario (table 9.3 and figure 9.5) levels off more quickly and at a lower level compared to that associated with the constant acquisition scenario (table 9.2 and figure 9.3).

It is important to remember that the underlying cohort-level dynamics are exactly the same in both scenarios (i.e., figures 9.1 and 9.2). Why are the aggregate retention rates so different? Under the growing acquisition scenario, a large proportion of the customer base at any time is made up of younger cohorts. Earlier on in a cohort's life, the cohort-level retention rates of those members who are still "alive" are lower than those observed later on in the cohort's life (figure 9.2). Because the aggregate retention rate is a weighted average of the cohort-specific retention rates, this lowers the overall retention rate.

We also note that once the firm has been operating for a number of periods, the aggregate retention rate levels off, which can lead

Figure 9.6. Comparing the Aggregate Retention Rates from the Two Growth Scenarios

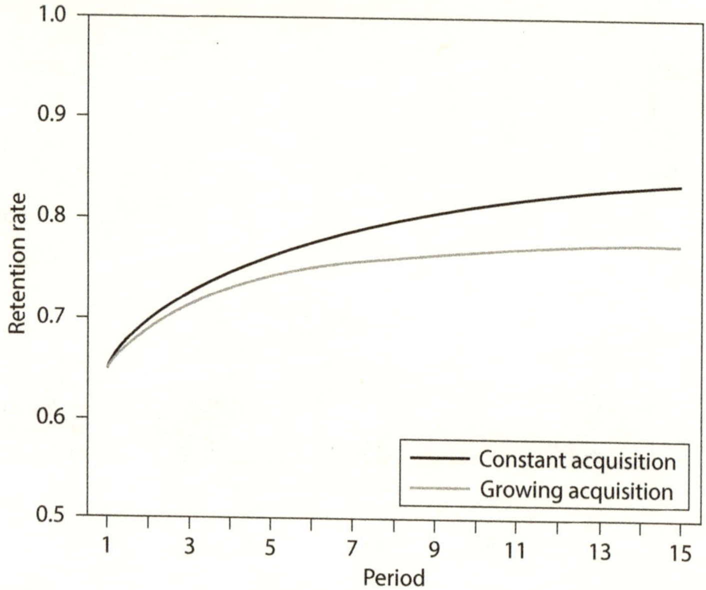

the uninformed observer to conclude that there is a constant retention (or churn) rate. This is contrary to the cohort-level dynamics observed in figure 9.2.

The key lesson is that aggregate measures of customer behavior computed off the whole customer base can be misleading when the mixing of different-aged cohorts hides cohort-level dynamics in the behavior of interest, similar to the point made in our discussion of table 7.5. Whenever possible, we should always start with cohort-level examinations and only aggregate across cohorts when we are confident that doing so will not lead to incorrect inferences about customer behavior.

Retention Reporting

In chapter 7 (Lens 5), we considered a plot of revenue broken down by acquisition cohort. Since the ability to track customers over time is built into contractual businesses, it should be a simple exercise to create such a plot. It is not uncommon to see such plots in the S-1 filings of SaaS companies. However, these plots must be consumed with care.

Figure 9.7 is one such plot for a hypothetical SaaS firm. The 2019 and 2020 revenue from the 2018 cohort are $22 million and $24 million, respectively. Such a firm will talk about 109% "net dollar retention" for this cohort from 2019 to 2020. Similarly, the 2019 and 2020 revenue for the 2019 cohort is $40 million in both years, a 100% "net dollar retention."

While such "retained revenue" is not to be scoffed at, the number should not be taken at face value. Does 100% retained revenue mean that no members of that cohort of customers churned and they spent the same amount over time, or did we lose half the cohort, but the spending of the remaining customers increased to recoup the lost revenue? Anyone interested in the health of the customer base will definitely want to know which of these two scenarios is behind the numbers. As such, it is vital to make use of a multiplicative

Figure 9.7. Annual Revenue by Cohort

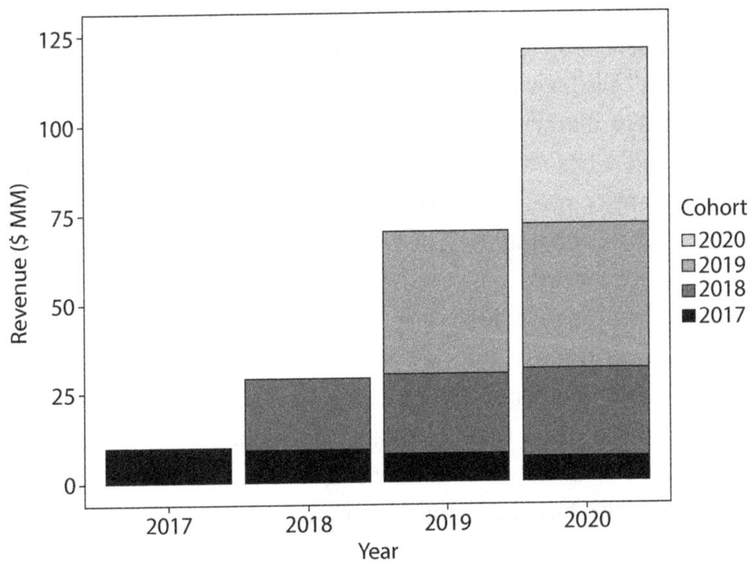

decomposition similar in spirit to those used in Lenses 3–5, but with some modifications.

We start with cohort revenue in period = number of cohort members still "alive" × average spend (given "alive"). In some settings, especially those related to communications, average spend given "alive" is called ARPU, average revenue per user.

This can be rewritten as cohort size × % cohort surviving × average spend (given "alive"). The big difference to the decomposition is that we are talking about the percentage of the cohort still alive as opposed to the percent active.

Whether and how to decompose average spend (given "alive") will depend on the context. For a software product, it may be number of users (or seats) × average price per user. If there are several tiers to the subscription, it may be useful to decompose it into the percent upgrading, downgrading, and remaining at the same level. Where the subscription provides "access" and the subscriber can buy additional services, it may be useful to analyze purchases in a similar manner to that used in chapter 8.

Be Wary of the "R" Word

We have been very careful in our use of the words "retained" and "retention." We have done so because we feel they are abused terms, being used to characterize quantities that are not equivalent. A quantity referred to as retention by one firm will often not be the same as the quantity referred to as retention by another firm. We even sometimes see it being used in different ways in the same presentation deck for a firm!

To be on the safe side, we would contend the term should only be used in contractual settings, as it is only in such settings that we know for sure whether or not the customer is still "alive." As observed in chapter 5, the fact that a customer does not make a purchase in one period in a noncontractual setting does not mean that they will not make a purchase in the next (more on that later).

Some people will call figure 9.1 a retention rate plot. This is bad practice, as the term "retention rate" has a well-established meaning, as illustrated in figure 9.2. If you call it a retention plot, make sure that you label the y-axis very carefully (e.g., "% cohort retained").

People tie themselves in all sorts of knots when using the term "retention" in noncontractual settings. It is not uncommon to see a plot of the percentage of a cohort that is still active (as explored in Lenses 3 through 5) called a "retention plot" or a "retention rate plot." As we have seen, someone who does not buy in one period (and is therefore not "retained") can buy in the next (and is therefore now "retained"). It does not make sense.

Returning to Madrigal, figure 9.8, which is a copy of a figure we saw earlier (figure 7.5), reports the evolution of the number of active customers by cohort. Focusing on the 2016 cohort, Madrigal acquired 1.49 million new customers in 2016; 413,000 members of the cohort made at least one purchase in 2017, and 344,000 members of the cohort made at least one purchase in 2018.

Figure 9.8. Evolution of the Number of Active Customers by Year of Acquisition

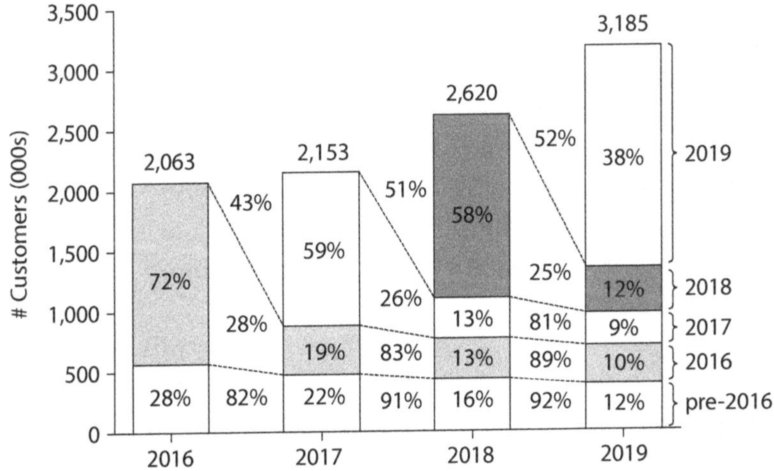

With reference to figure 9.8, some people would say that Madrigal retained 28% of the 2016 cohort in 2017. In a narrow sense, that is correct. However, we have a well-established name for that quantity. As discussed in chapter 7, it is called a repeat-buying rate.

We also see from figure 9.8 that the number of 2016 cohort members active in 2018 is 83% of the number active in 2017. Some people will call this an 83% retention rate. However, some of the 334,000 customers active in 2018 were not active in 2017, so it makes no sense to say that 83% of the customers were retained.

We strongly advise you to only use the words "retained" and "retention" if you operate in a contractual setting and, even then, to use the terms carefully.

Different Notions of Customer Acquisition

Until now, we have taken the view that a customer is acquired when they make their first purchase. However, there may be a number of key events on the path to the first purchase (if ever) that are of interest to your firm.

This is perhaps most evident in the apps space. In a dating app, key events are installing the app, registering, and subscribing to the service. At which point is the customer "acquired"?

Not everyone who installs the app will register. Not everyone who registers will take out a subscription. Recall that in Lens 3 we looked at the distribution of the time between a customer's first purchase and their second purchase (if ever). It is therefore useful to look at the distribution of the time between, say, install and register, and register and subscribe. The specific events to consider will depend on the exact nature of the onboarding funnel relevant to your firm.

If you have a freemium business model, it is very likely the case that a large proportion of your users never make a purchase. (The exact proportion will depend a lot on the type of freemium service you operate.) You will be interested in the time from first using the service to making a purchase (if ever). The purchasing behavior of those ever making a purchase can be studied using the various analyses outlined in the previous chapters.

Quantities of Interest Other than Spend

In many online settings, usage of the service is a key quantity of interest. The exact same logic of our analyses of revenue and profit can be applied to analyze usage.

For example, the time spent on an app during a day by an active user can be decomposed as the number of sessions × average number of minutes per session, and variability in these quantities across users tracked over time.

The usage of the features in an app can be analyzed in a similar manner to that used to analyze customers' purchasing of products, as examined in chapter 8.

Beyond app usage, other forms of user engagement can be analyzed in an audit. For instance, posting reviews (or other kinds of content on social media) could be viewed as "transactions," and then the length of these posts could be explored in the same way we treated spend.

Other Dimensions

The starting point for the idea of the customer-base audit was to note that, at the simplest level, a transaction can be characterized on three dimensions: customer, time, and product.

These are not the only dimensions that may be of interest. In some settings, a transaction can also be tagged by a channel dimension. For example, for an omni-channel retailer, was this an online or in-store purchase? For an online purchase, another dimension would be the device used (e.g., PC, tablet, phone). Understanding the evolution of customers' purchasing across different channels/devices is of strategic importance to many businesses.

The customer can also be tagged with various attributes. For example, via what channel were they acquired? While it may be too detailed for a high-level customer-base audit, further defining cohorts not just by the time of acquisition but also channel of acquisition can be a very insightful analysis. How do customers acquired via different channels differ in terms of the evolution of their buying behavior? Some businesses will have demographic information on their customers (or "firmographic" information in B2B settings). Customer segments can be created on the basis of these variables, and the behavior of customers analyzed separately by segment.

Conclusion

We have identified some of the key changes or additional analyses that may be required when conducting a customer-base audit as we move away from classic noncontractual business settings. We hope we have addressed any questions you had as we developed the Lenses 1 through 5 analyses using the running example of Madrigal.

If there are questions remaining, we encourage you to step back and reflect on the principles underpinning all the analyses presented in this book. We have focused on the customer dimension of behavior recorded in the firm's databases. We have looked at the idea of decompositions, be they additive or multiplicative. We have looked at the need to recognize inter-customer differences, represented using distributions and decile analyses. We have explored the importance of focusing on cohorts of customers, recognizing that when creating cohorts, the fundamental defining characteristic is the timing of the customer's "birth." Reflect on how you can take the principles and apply them to the situation you are facing. Doing so will provide a new perspective on how to understand the performance of your firm from the perspective of the customer.

Conclusion
From Audit to Action

Imagine looking at your business under a microscope. That is what a customer-base audit is like: It provides deep insight into customer differences and dynamics that have always been there but were typically not visible. On seeing an audit of her customer base, one CEO remarked that it was like looking at the "heartbeat of her business." This reaction is typical because the audit gives business leaders an entirely new perspective—insight that either did not exist before or was buried deep within an analytics group, but never seen by key decision makers.

In the introduction, we defined a customer-centric firm as one that:

- views the customer as the fundamental unit of analysis;
- has (customer) acquisition, retention, and development at the core of its (organic) growth accounting framework;
- makes decisions through the lens of (long-term) customer profitability; and
- recognizes—and acts on—the fact that not all customers are equal.

The increasing speed of business and competitive dynamics now makes this shift to customer centricity a necessity. In all industries, there is (or at least should be) a "land grab" for high-value customers. Successful businesses (growing profitably and meeting or beating business plans) need to understand the drivers of growth to ensure they keep doing the things that have led to their success. Struggling businesses, on the other hand, need to understand what has caused the issues to ensure they solve the right problem.

The customer-base audit will frame the problem you are trying to solve, highlighting bite-sized issues and opportunities that can be understood and improved. And this is very much a whole-company problem. Too often, businesses view all things customer related as a marketing issue alone. In practice, creating a customer-centric mind-set should be at the heart of how the entire enterprise is run.

Many businesses talk eloquently about embracing customer centricity but are only scratching the surface of what is possible. They might understand the rationale, but many are failing to act or even grasp the full potential of customer-centric change.

Why is using a customer-base audit to catalyze change so difficult? There are many reasons for this:

- Businesses have developed customer proxies (e.g., stores) that have been seen as "good enough" or are fixated on a specific customer segmentation scheme.
- Businesses have not had the data to enable customer-level insights or the technology to take customer-level actions.
- Businesses see the change as a "marketing problem."

Next Steps: How to Go from Audit to Action

In our experience, there are multiple coherent paths to follow. However, *the key is to translate the customer-base audit into a set of customer strategies.* You want to move from blunt and broadcast actions to surgical micro-segments and customer-level actions. You also need to apply a customer lens to decisions across the firm. Sometimes, this will simply validate existing approaches (and give confidence to amplify and accelerate existing activities). But often a customer lens will cause the business to take a radically different approach.

This chapter is structured around three core elements of a customer-centric strategy:

1. Customer-centric planning: how to create a business plan that has the insights and implications from the customer-base audit at its heart.
2. Customer acquisition: how to acquire the right quantity and quality of customers and ensure that acquisition spend is aligned to customer value.
3. Customer retention and development: how to look after the customers you already have and ensure your investment in them is aligned to current and potential value.

The rest of the chapter is focused on bringing to life practical examples of how the customer-base audit translates into real business value.

Customer-Centric Planning

All businesses have a plan. Traditionally, a plan is built up by product line, channel or geography. We urge you to consider a customer plan as a new (and increasingly critical) dimension of planning. What does this mean? Put simply, it is about understanding how much of your revenue and profit will come from existing customers and how many new customers are required to "fill the gap." Taking this approach is a critical sanity check (or better yet, starting point).

Once you have determined how much revenue and profit you expect to get from your existing customers (retention), and consequently how many new customers you need to attract to deliver on your business plan (acquisition), you need to make customer performance part of the operating rhythm of the business. Keeping track of the divergences (both positive and negative) from this plan is a great way to course correct before there is a material issue. If a plan has been missed, you need to establish whether that was driven by acquisition or retention, and—if retention—whether that was driven by recent cohorts or all cohorts. These simple insights are critical to "solving the right problem" and avoiding the gravitational pull of blunt promotional levers to get back on track.

Industry Examples: Why Looking at Your Customer Base Is Crucial

A private equity business had invested in an online retailer in Africa and bought into an aggressive business plan. They undertook a Lens 5 analysis and started looking at customer cohorts and unbundling the revenue that was being generated from existing versus new customers. That exercise quickly led to the realization that they would need to acquire more than 100% of the population of the country to achieve the plan!

A luxury British department store was analyzing the performance of their top-spending customers (those who were spending more than £5,000 a year). Initially, they were delighted to observe that the number of high-spending customers had increased from 412 last year to over 1,000 this year. However, this initial excitement was offset when they conducted a Lens 2 analysis and discovered that over half the 412 had stopped shopping with them. When they started to dig further and looked at the nationality of these high-spend customers, they discovered that most of the "lost" customers were Chinese, and this directly correlated with a fall in the RMB–GBP exchange rate: When the exchange rate moved, the attractiveness of shopping in the UK shifted. This was a critical piece of information because it enabled the business to develop a much more nuanced plan that was sensitive to key exchange rates.

Segmenting your customer base

Most businesses with a customer base have some default segmentation scheme based on customer personas or behavioral (e.g., RFM) segments. These segmentation schemes are often very powerful sources of insight that can help develop targeted marketing messages and CRM activities. However, the challenge of planning based on this type of segmentation is that the members of the segments change over time, which makes it almost impossible to discern the underlying factors driving performance. For this reason, we think of cohorts (Lens 3) as foundational; the membership of a cohort is fixed, and so behavior over time is much easier to understand. It is not that other groupings of customers are unhelpful; it is just they are not helpful for planning in the absence of a cohort-based perspective.

Customer Acquisition

The customer-base audit highlights many critical aspects of customer acquisition. First, Lens 5 emphasizes the need to acquire new customers to drive growth. With very few exceptions, most businesses see declining revenue from existing cohorts, which means that acquiring new customers is fundamental to long-term growth. But as we see from Lens 1, customers are not created equal: It is important to understand how to align acquisition spend with customer value. Finally, Lens 3 highlights that customer value evolves over time, which requires firms to think about a customer payback. This section is organized into four parts:

1. Aligning acquisition to time of year
2. Products aligned to acquisition
3. Aligning acquisition spend to customer value
4. Acquiring customers, not transactions

1. Aligning acquisition to time of year

Our Lens 4 and 5 analyses show how acquisition varies over time, which can highlight some interesting opportunities. In the audit we looked at quarterly data, but it is important to note that opportunities are often revealed as one digs deeper. This is a common and important theme: The customer-base audit will shine a light on opportunities and challenges, but one typically needs to further analyze to get to insights that drive action. In these examples, it is the granular view of acquisition—by month or even week—that highlights opportunities. The value comes from asking why and being ready to deep dive into the detail.

Industry Examples: How Customer Data Can Reveal the Unexpected

A train ticketing business was reviewing the volume and quality of customers acquired throughout the year and noticed a significant spike of high-value customers coming through in September. They initially thought it was an anomaly, but when they started digging deeper and running focus groups to actually talk to these customers, they realized there was a surge in new students (and parents of students) who were buying books of train tickets before they went to college. This insight led them to create a new marketing campaign focused on attracting this particular group.

A major US theme park observed large numbers of new customers who visited their theme parks with children when they would have expected those children to be in school. When they drilled down into the data, they discovered a number of interesting subgroups of customers, both international families and also US children at schools with nonstandard holidays. This led to a strategy targeting families with children interested in visiting the park at unexpected times.

2. Products aligned to customer acquisition

As we saw when we reintroduced the product dimension in chapter 8, categories (and subcategories, products, and brands) play different roles in the customer life cycle. By understanding the value associated with different products, businesses can make intelligent investments in range, price or availability aligned to customer value. In all these examples, a Lens 1 analysis highlights the distribution of customer value, and then motivates the leadership to ask questions about which brands and categories are acquiring and retaining these customers.

Industry Examples: How a Customer Lens Leads to Surprising Business Decisions

A UK department store was looking at what product categories were favored by high-value customers in their first transaction. At one extreme, they observed that customers who came in to buy televisions, typically only bought televisions. But customers who came in to buy beds were also buying mattresses, pillowcases, and bedroom furniture. The insight—supported by talking to customers—was that bed purchases were an indicator of customers refurbishing a room and were trigger purchases for significant downstream spend. This conclusion led them to price beds at relatively low margin and use them to acquire potential high-value customers.

Figleaves was a multi-brand lingerie retailer; one of its key brands was La Perla, a premium Italian lingerie brand. A new merchandising leader undertook a review of brand profitability and saw that La Perla was loss-making—it had relatively low margin, a high returns rate, and expensive photography costs. However, when they looked at La Perla through the lens of their customers, it was often the first brand purchased by their most valuable customers. This is a good example of a "sign flip" decision. If you were looking at the brand through a traditional P&L lens, you would decide to delist it. But looking at the same brand through the customer lens would lead to a diametrically opposite decision. As a result of this insight, Figleaves expanded its range of La Perla, and this was a critical driver of the online retailer's early growth.

A European maternity retailer saw that a well-known baby-bottle brand was a great way to acquire high-value customers, but they had recently seen a number of new entrants into their market discounting the brand. The retailer, which was the market leader, was able to negotiate exclusivity with the brand owner and structure a deal that only made sense because of the downstream customer value that was being acquired.

3. Aligning acquisition spend to customer value

Lens 4 highlights that cohorts acquired at different times can have different value. But, as noted in chapter 9, cohorts do not only have to be defined based on time alone. In this section, we are comparing cohorts acquired at the same time but also via different marketing channels. We see many businesses spending marketing dollars (particularly digital marketing) on the basis of an "average" customer, which we now know does not exist. And we see significant opportunities to align marketing spend to customer value. In the first example, the channel is newspaper, and in the second, keyword.

Industry Examples: Customer Value Across Different Channels

A UK pay-TV service was looking at the customers who were being acquired through different marketing channels. They observed that the acquisition cost of customers via advertising in the *Times* newspaper was about four times that of the *Sun* newspaper. Their initial thought was to move all their marketing spend to the *Sun*. However, when they looked at customers' value to date, they saw that the value of customers being acquired through the *Times* was five times higher than via the *Sun*. So, in fact, their strategy ended up being the complete opposite.

A UK retailer was spending £20 million a year on Google paid search across several thousand keywords. At an aggregate level they observed an average customer acquisition cost of £12 and an average customer value to date of £95. This insight gave them confidence to start scaling their spend. However, when they drilled down to look at the performance of each keyword, they saw a completely different picture. At the keyword level, the vast majority had customer acquisition costs of more than £30. And when they looked at the distribution of customer value to date, most of their customers had a value of less than £30. The aggregated average numbers gave a completely misleading picture of performance, and the sad conclusion was that most of their money was being spent acquiring customers at a cost greater than their value.

4. Acquiring customers, not transactions—look beyond that first purchase

Lands' End—the US mail-order retailer—was famous for claiming, "You're not a customer until you've made two purchases." Its customer acquisition team was focused not just on bringing in new customers, but on ensuring people made a second purchase. This is a fantastic insight that recognizes the ease—particularly in the digital world—of "buying" transactions with aggressive promotions. Focusing on the first two purchases drives a more thoughtful approach. Success here is based on a structured and focused program (often called a welcome or nursery program) that encourages customer loyalty or greater self-selection by more valuable customers.

Industry Examples: Granular Customer Detail
A UK online retailer was achieving new customer targets but found it was delivering lackluster top-line sales a few months later. A Lens 3 analysis highlighted that it had attracted the wrong type of customer. The retailer had used extreme promotional marketing techniques that had delivered the revenue and initial customer numbers but had failed to attract loyal consumers that would spend more in the long run. It was essentially acquiring transactions rather than customers.

Another UK retailer looked at the length of time between a customer's first and second purchases. It observed that half of the customers who made a second purchase did so in less than eight weeks (until this point, they had arbitrarily selected six months as the boundary for deciding that a new customer was lapsing). This insight led to a new-customer strategy dubbed internally as "back in 8." The retailer designed several clever mechanics—some promotional, others not—to secure a quick second purchase.

Customer Retention and Development

Once you have acquired customers, the key is to develop strategies that drive engagement and incremental profitability. However, developing the right game plan is a significant management challenge. Many businesses talk about completely personalized customer strategies, but the reality today is there are substantial data, technology, and resource constraints.

So, in practice, businesses need to develop a road map and focus on the most important strategies first. And the customer-base audit is critical to determining where to concentrate your efforts. For all businesses, there is an option to "do nothing," to simply let customer behavior evolve naturally. But the ticket to long-term success is to make surgical interventions that drive incremental value. The four crucial steps you need to take to achieve this are:

1. Invest in the proposition based on customer value.
2. Invest in VIP customers.
3. Nudge customers to increase profit.
4. Manage loss-making customers.

1. Invest in the customer proposition based on customer value

These ideas highlight the value of looking at different elements of your proposition—service, product, experience, pricing—through the customer lens, to understand what is important to your highest-value customers. The investment in your offer needs to be proportionate with the potential customer value.

Industry Examples: Deep Diving into Customer Behavior

In these examples, a Lens 1 or Lens 2 analysis motivated the leadership to want to understand who their highest-value customers actually were, and what was important to them. The examples also highlight that some of the insights are purely data-driven whereas others require talking to customers.

A UK shirt brand was evaluating the profitability of its stores based on a traditional "four walls" profit (the revenue through the till, and direct costs of the store). This analysis highlighted that a number of stores were simply not profitable. However, when the business overlaid the numbers with customer data and looked at the role that stores were playing to acquire and retain customers, they reached a completely different conclusion. They found large numbers of customers had made their first purchase in a store and then subsequently bought online. They also found some people were spending considerable amounts online but were frequently coming into the store to try on new products. This analysis led to the creation of a "360-degree" view of profit, in which stores were evaluated based on the profitability of all customers who touched the store. It led to a radically different store rollout plan.

The following examples highlight where more in-depth focus groups were required to really understand what was driving customer behavior. A low-cost UK fashion retailer had brought in a new design team. The business talked to customers and—based on their feedback—decided to make its range much younger and more fashionable. Unfortunately, the new range led to a slump in profits and revenue. The business had failed to grasp that the customers they had spoken to might have been the types of customers they wanted but they were not the customers who generated the bulk of the profits. Understanding who your core customers are is crucial.

A US retailer was focused on diagnosing why their "one-and-done" customers were turning away from the brand. It found that the delivery experience was the single biggest cause of their failure to make a second purchase. The action was to remove budget from retention promotions and extend its warehouse operating hours to improve the delivery experience. This is a great example of the need to think cross-silo to solve the problem. Of course, few marketing directors like to see their budgets reduced.

A US hotel chain was researching what was important to different high-value customer segments. It found that it had a significant group of tradesmen (e.g., electricians, plumbers) for whom secure parking was extremely important because they left valuable tools in their pickups. Up until this point, they had seen secure parking as a cost with unclear benefit and it was relatively low on the list of hotel enhancements. Once they overlaid the potential incremental downstream value from this customer segment, it became one of the top-priority projects to roll out across the estate.

A pay-TV service in Europe had a high churn rate and was investing heavily to win back customers. But this strategy was proving expensive and unsuccessful. When it ran focus groups and talked to customers about the causes of churn, a large percentage of them revealed they were unhappy with the quality of their set-top boxes. This led the business to pivot, removing money from marketing promotions and investing it in developing and offering customers better-quality set-top boxes. Customer satisfaction improved, churn reduced, and the overall profitability of the business improved dramatically.

2. Invest in VIP customers

VIP customers are a critical feature of most businesses. Understanding who these customers are, what they love, and where they come from is an integral part of driving growth. A good mental model here is a "customer P&L" in which one can invest in a customer aligned to their potential value.

An online luxury retailer performed a Lens 1 decile analysis and discovered the top 2% of customers were responsible for 50% of revenue and 70% of profit. A typical high-value customer was spending 25 times more than an average customer, and 100 times more than a low-value customer. This led to the creation of a VIP program that has been a significant part of the company's growth and success. The VIP program had a number of elements (and interestingly, the customers were not told they were VIPs). One example was a "top of queue" experience: all emails or orders from VIP customers went straight to the front of the queue, delivering an exceptionally high-service experience. Another example was a sale preview concept wherein VIP customers were offered access to the seasonal sales 48 hours in advance. It is worth noting that both these ideas had a high perceived value but low marginal cost.

Later, the company introduced a fast-track program to identify potential VIP customers based on their first few purchases, and automatically give them VIP status. One famous example was identifying customers who had spent $300 on a plain white T-shirt!

3. Nudge customers to increase profit

For the majority of customers, the challenge is to keep them active and to nudge them to higher profit over time. As we saw from the profit decile change table (chapter 4, table 4.2), a significant percentage of the customer base is reasonably engaged with Madrigal, but its spend and profit can vary significantly from year to year. The challenge here is to design surgical—and often clever and creative—campaigns to nudge customers. One more purchase, one more category, can drive a significant overall impact.

Industry Examples: Why Loyal, Active Customers Stop Buying Frequently

An online retailer had grown consistently for many years by simply increasing their product range, but this strategy was now seeing diminishing returns, and growth was beginning to plateau. However, a Lens 5 analysis revealed that they had lots of loyal, active customers who were not buying frequently. They realized that "nudging" these customers to make one additional purchase per year would have a dramatic impact on their overall growth. They developed a "plus one" campaign focused on getting customers to make one additional purchase using creative CRM strategies that sent personalized messages and promotions based on the individual customer's buying and browsing history.

A luxury brand undertook a Lens 1 analysis and found a significant group of high-value customers who were buying at an average 20% discount. They had previously hypothesized that they had "full price" customers, and "discount" customers, but the reality was that a significant group of customers was buying both full price and discount. On drilling further, they saw two distinct subgroups: a group who bought everything on a small discount of around 20% and another group that bought at full price and clearance. This insight allowed them to create clever strategies aligned to these quite different shopping behaviors.

4. Manage loss-making customers

There are critical insights that come from understanding customer profit versus revenue. We typically find groups of loss-making customers, and strategies are required to either stop selling to them or mitigate the losses. We discussed the different "levels" of profit in chapter 2—ranging from simply considering direct product costs to a fully costed analysis. In practice, as you refine your measure of profit, you will invariably identify more unprofitable customers.

Industry Examples: How to Spot Loss-Making Customers
A major UK supermarket discovered many loss-making customers when they started looking at profit deciles rather than revenue deciles. One customer had made a loss of more than £120,000 over a three-year period. It turned out the retailer was often launching new PlayStation games as loss leaders to drive foot traffic into stores. Online, they had limited customers to buying a maximum of five units per order of each game, but this customer had placed more than 11,000 orders and was then reselling the products. The inconvenient truth was that the online team had focused too much attention on revenue and had not spotted the trend for abusive loss-making customers. There is now a limit on the total number of units of a product ordered, not just in an individual order. The business also monitors loss-making customers on a weekly basis.

A US fashion retailer had always been focused on analyzing product return rates but had never looked at customers' return rates. By looking at customer-level returns, they identified a small group of customers (<1%) who were responsible for 40% of all returns, and this included an abusive subgroup of 100% returners who became known as "free rental" customers. The immediate action was to stop marketing to them.

An Australian retailer looked at the distribution of customer profitability and discovered a significant group of customers who only bought on promotions (subsequently branded as "Discount Doras"). Rather than seeing this as a problem, they proactively engaged with these customers to get rid of clearance inventory.

Some Words of Caution

We believe that the approach presented in the book is foundational. But we are equally cognizant of companies/sectors that have developed around other kinds of customer analysis, and so we finish with some notes of caution.

Beware segments versus cohorts

Most businesses that have any customer relationships will have some customer segmentation—this might be based on a loyalty status such as gold, silver, or bronze; recency–frequency status; or a persona-based segmentation. These are valuable for marketing strategies and operations. However, they can be problematic when it comes to diagnosing performance. The main issue with all these segmentation schemes is that, unlike cohorts, they are not necessarily persistent: Customers can move between segments.

For example, when a business sees that its gold customers are performing well, it needs to understand the performance of new-to-the-business gold customers and existing gold customers, but also the migration of customers from bronze to silver to gold. This rapidly drives huge analytical complexity, as well as confusion for the decision makers trying to leverage the segmentation scheme. Segmentation can be a useful "overlay" on top of a cohort-based approach, which can help put into practice the insights from the customer-base audit. But it is not a substitute. Whether segmentation is used or not, a cohort approach is the foundational way to understand customer behavior.

To add to the confusion, many people misuse the term "cohort," often implying that it is interchangeable with "segment." We see the following as the simplest definitions:

- Cohort—a group of customers acquired in the same period, which could be a week, month, quarter, or year.
- Cohort + attribute(s)—a group of customers acquired in the same period who share one or more attributes. For example, the 2019 Facebook cohort would include all customers acquired via Facebook in 2019.
- Segment—a group of customers, usually regardless of time of acquisition, that share a common characteristic or set of characteristics.

Beware unusual analyses and metrics

Beware of analyses that appear confusing. We see many businesses that quote impressive-sounding metrics, including sales retention rates, new-to-repeat-customer sales conversion, and customer churn rates. These are often meaningless when data is overly aggregated, impossible to interpret without context, or simply need to be precisely defined. For public companies, such metrics are often more about "telling a story" than truly helping investors understand the fundamentals. When this is being done internally, we strongly advise you to (i) map onto the analyses we have presented here, and (ii) track alongside more fundamental cohort measures. We love when businesses quote the formula when presenting any nonobvious customer metrics. Finally, never be embarrassed to ask the source of data and precise calculation, particularly for a metric that you have never seen before.

Audit first, models later

Seek first to understand. We often see businesses jumping to build models for churn prediction, customer lifetime value estimation, or personalized "next-best-offer" suggestions before undertaking basic analyses. We often see this kind of premature move toward models as a solution in search of a problem. There is no question that building customer models as part of the customer analytics process is key to putting the insights from the audit into practice, but they are not a starting point. Unfortunately, it is typical that data scientists are frequently drawn to build models before (or instead of) doing basic (descriptive) analysis, but you will always build a better model if you start from a clear baseline and a firm understanding of the problem you are trying to solve.

Earlier in the book, we described our work as "unashamedly descriptive," and we hope the reader has come to understand and appreciate this term. That is not to criticize models as essential components in the overall tool kit—we are proud to be modelers ourselves! It is just a question of sequence and priority, and we feel that good descriptive work often takes a back seat to a modeling exercise.

Where do you start?

We see different starting points: There is either a specific symptom or business problem—for example, our growth has slowed, we have missed our plans, we want to launch a new loyalty program—that lends itself to a focused set of analyses that will typically be aligned to one or more of the five lenses. Alternatively, a leadership team may want to do a deep dive to understand what is happening to their customer base. Or there may be natural curiosity to simply understand how customers differ from each other and over time.

The analyses we have presented are tried and tested but are by no means exhaustive. They are a starting point. For many firms they will be enough, but others will want to dig deeper.

The volume of analyses in this book may seem overwhelming, but once you have the data in the right form, we see this as no more than one or two sprints for an experienced data scientist. As a benchmark, Bruce and Michael run a hackathon with their MBA class in which teams of four students are given a customer data set at 8 a.m.

and need to perform a customer-base audit within 12 hours. It never ceases to amaze us how much can be achieved by a focused team with a deadline and good guidance.

The New Operating Mindset

Many companies talk about being customer centric but keep making the same decisions with the same logic, in the same silos and with the same incentives. How can they be surprised when nothing changes? We are not saying there is a single prescriptive framework. Instead, we are urging you to consider the customer-base audit as a catalyst for change, shifting mindsets and giving business leaders a new perspective to drive transformation.

A quote from the *Harvard Business Review* articulates what we believe is a good formula:

> Most successful transformations begin with small groups that are loosely connected but united by a shared purpose. They're made of people who are already enthusiastic about the initiative but are willing to test assumptions and, later, to recruit their peers. Leaders can give voice to that shared purpose and help those small groups connect, but the convincing has to be done on the ground. Unless people feel that they own the effort, it's not likely to go very far.[12]

The key to this sort of customer-centric change is to inspire people to think differently, to be curious about customer data, and to see the customer-base audit as the first step on the journey to customer centricity.

Notes

1 For an excellent elaboration of these ideas, see the "Executive Summary" of Tim Ambler, *Marketing and the Bottom Line*, 2nd ed. (London: FT Prentice Hall, 2003). Tim defines marketing as "the sourcing and harvesting of inward cash flow" (294), which is a view that we embrace.

2 Lisa Kart, Alexander Linden, and W. Roy Schulte (2013), *Extend Your Portfolio of Analytics Capabilities*, Gartner, 3.

3 Oxford Dictionaries, Oxford University Press, https://premium.oxforddictionaries.com/us/definition/american_english/customer.

4 Note that the sums of the individual elements of the table may not equal the reported row or column totals due to rounding.

5 Since AOF is defined as average order frequency *among buyers*, its lower bound is 1.0 (i.e., if every buyer made exactly one purchase).

6 When creating this plot, we do not pay attention to the point in calendar time at which the customer made their purchase. We are only interested in the time between purchases. For example, someone who made their second purchase on the first day of Q4/2018 and their third purchase eight weeks later is treated the same as someone who made their second purchase in the second week of Q1/2016 and their third purchase eight weeks later.

7 Within the new product sales forecasting literature, these are called depth of repeat curves. The seminal paper in this area is Gerald J. Eskin, "Dynamic Forecasts of New Product Demand Using a Depth of Repeat Model," *Journal of Marketing Research*, 10 (May 1973), 115–29.

8 There is nothing magical about our choice of four bins for each of R, F, and M and associated bin boundaries. The choices should be made so as to maximize the insight for the recipient of this analysis. Having said that, we feel that it makes sense to have stand-alone recency bins for the first and last quarters. Similarly, it makes sense to have a frequency = 1 bin.

9 Even if you have complete records for every single customer from the day your firm started, you may choose to have a "pre-20xy" cohort to make the various plots that follow more legible. Besides, long after the shakeout (described in chapter 5) takes place, the distinctions between cohorts are less meaningful and interesting. The benefits arising from tracking old cohorts as separate entities will often not be worth the effort to do so.

10 See https://thetaclv.com/resource/c3/ for an introduction.

11 If a new cohort contains a large number of reacquired customers, it can be a good idea to examine separately the behavior of the truly new versus the reacquired customers to see if there are any differences (e.g., do the reacquired customers churn at a higher or lower rate?).

12 Greg Satell, "4 Tips for Managing Organizational Change," *Harvard Business Review*, August 27, 2019, https://hbr.org/2019/08/4-tips-for-managing-organizational-change.

Index

Note: Page numbers in italics indicate figures or tables

About the Authors

Peter Fader is the Frances and Pei-Yuan Chia Professor of Marketing at the Wharton School of the University of Pennsylvania. His expertise centers on the analysis of behavioral data to understand and forecast customer shopping/purchasing activities. He works with firms from a wide range of industries, such as telecommunications, financial services, gaming/entertainment, retailing, and pharmaceuticals.

In addition to his various roles and responsibilities at Wharton, Fader cofounded a predictive analytics firm (Zodiac) in 2015, which was sold to Nike in 2018. He then cofounded (and continues to run) Theta to commercialize his more recent work on "customer-based corporate valuation."

Fader is the author of *Customer Centricity: Focus on the Right Customers for Strategic Advantage* (2020, 2012) and coauthor of *The Customer Centricity Playbook* (2018) with Sarah Toms. He has won many awards for his research and teaching accomplishments.

Bruce G. S. Hardie is a professor of marketing at London Business School. For most of his career, his research has focused on developing tools for analyzing customer and marketing data. He has worked with market research firms and their clients on the development of marketing analytics solutions for new product sales forecasting and marketing mix analysis. He has collaborated extensively with Peter Fader, developing a number of key customer analytics tools for computing customer lifetime value (CLV) that have been used by thousands of data scientists and researchers around the world. He teaches courses on customer and marketing analytics, and the data-driven enterprise.

Michael Ross is a data agitator. He is the senior vice president of retail data science at EDITED and a non-executive director at Sainsbury's Bank, Domestic & General, and N Brown Group. He has cofounded businesses including eCommera, DynamicAction, and figleaves.com, and was also a consultant at McKinsey & Company. Michael has an MA in mathematics from the University of Cambridge. He is an Executive Fellow at London Business School and is on the commercial board of the Turing Institute.

WHARTON SCHOOL PRESS

About Wharton School Press

Wharton School Press, the book publishing arm of the Wharton School of the University of Pennsylvania, was established to inspire bold, insightful thinking within the global business community.

Wharton School Press publishes a select list of award-winning, best-selling, and thought-leading books that offer trusted business knowledge to help leaders at all levels meet the challenges of today and the opportunities of tomorrow. Led by a spirit of innovation and experimentation, Wharton School Press leverages groundbreaking digital technologies and has pioneered a fast-reading business-book format that fits readers' busy lives, allowing them to swiftly emerge with the tools and information needed to make an impact. Wharton School Press books offer guidance and inspiration on a variety of topics, including leadership, management, strategy, innovation, entrepreneurship, finance, marketing, social impact, public policy, and more.

Wharton School Press also operates an online bookstore featuring a curated selection of influential books by Wharton School faculty and Press authors published by a wide range of leading publishers.

To find books that will inspire and empower you to increase your impact and expand your personal and professional horizons, visit wsp.wharton.upenn.edu.

Wharton
UNIVERSITY *of* PENNSYLVANIA

About the Wharton School

Founded in 1881 as the world's first collegiate business school, the Wharton School of the University of Pennsylvania is shaping the future of business by incubating ideas, driving insights, and creating leaders who change the world. With a faculty of more than 235 renowned professors, Wharton has 5,000 undergraduate, MBA, executive MBA, and doctoral students. Each year 13,000 professionals from around the world advance their careers through Wharton Executive Education's individual, company-customized, and online programs. More than 100,000 Wharton alumni form a powerful global network of leaders who transform business every day. For more information, visit www.wharton.upenn.edu.

CPSIA information can be obtained
at www.ICGtesting.com
Printed in the USA
BVHW040221151022
649369BV00001BA/2

9 781613 631614